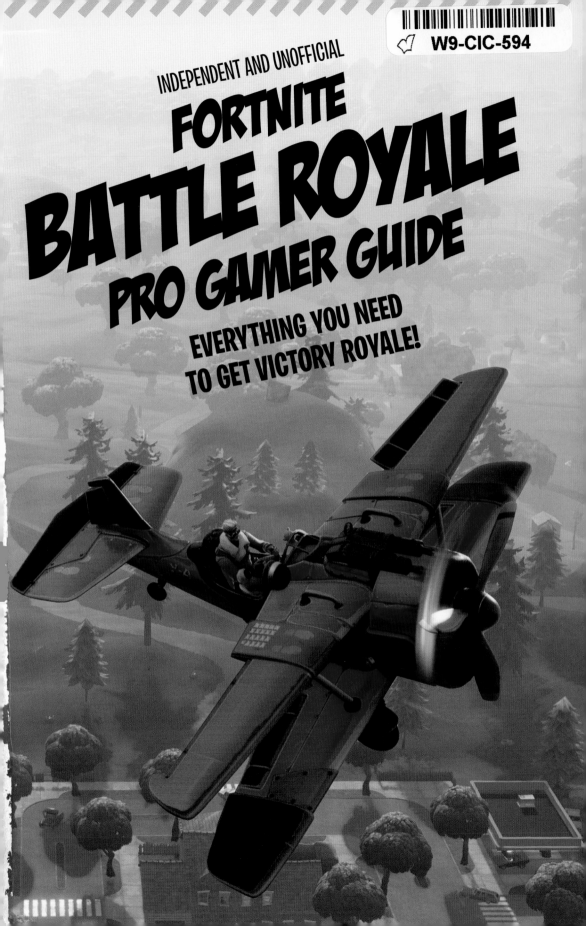

INDEPENDENT AND UNOFFICIAL

FORTNITE
BATTLE ROYALE
PRO GAMER GUIDE

EVERYTHING YOU NEED
TO GET VICTORY ROYALE!

THIS IS A CARLTON BOOK
Published in 2019 by Carlton Books Limited, an imprint of the Carlton Publishing Group,
20 Mortimer Street, London W1T 3JW
Text and design © Carlton Books Limited 2019
This book is not endorsed by Epic Games, Inc.
All information correct as of January 2019.

All screenshots and images of Fortnite characters/gameplay © Epic Games, Inc.

The publishers would like to thank the following sources for their kind permission to reproduce
the pictures in this book: Page 14: Patchra Suttivirat/Shutterstock; 15B: Roman Kosolapov/
Shutterstock; 16T: yudhiagust/Shutterstock; 157R: fim.design/Shutterstock; 160: Oleg Krugliak/
Shutterstock; 161T: Ekkaphan Chimpalee/Shutterstock; 164-165: Roman Kosolapov/Shutterstock;
176-177: fim.design/Shutterstock

Every effort has been made to acknowledge correctly and contact the source and/or copyright
holder of each picture and Carlton Books Limited apologises for any unintentional errors of
omissions, which will be corrected in future editions of this book.

ISBN: 978 1 78739 292 2
Printed in Dongguan, China
10 9 8 7 6 5 4 3 2

Designed and packaged by: Dynamo Limited
Written by: Kevin Pettman
Managing Art Editor: Matt Drew
Editorial Manager: Joff Brown
Production: Nicola Davey

INDEPENDENT AND UNOFFICIAL

FORTNITE
BATTLE ROYALE
PRO GAMER GUIDE

EVERYTHING YOU NEED
TO GET VICTORY ROYALE!

CARLTON
BOOKS

CONTENTS

BUILDING

Spot the shiny silver Loot Llama

Fortnite players **dream** of being in the right place when a **Loot Llama** appears, but can you find this silver llama **hidden** in the pages of this book?

INTRODUCTION

Listen up, Fortnite fans - you're about to become the Battle Royale boss! This epic guide will turn you into the ultimate pro gamer and reveal the top tactics, techniques and tips you need to clinch victory on the island. To be the last person standing in Fortnite, you've got to be brave, skilful, adventurous and dedicated. Are you ready to be the best?

FORTNITE FACT!

Since Epic Games released Fortnite **Battle Royale** in 2017, it's had over 140 million downloads to become one of the most popular video games EVER!

SAFETY FIRST

Fortnite Battle Royale can be played on **Xbox, PlayStation, PC, Switch,** and some tablets and mobiles. It's an online game, which means it requires an internet connection, and players of different ages from around the world compete against each other. Players with headsets and microphones can chat to each other, but this function can be turned off. Parents and guardians should always talk to children about **staying safe online** and encourage them to speak out if something happens that's upsetting. **See pages 24-27** for more safety advice.

Even if you're new to the frantic world of Fortnite, this book will soon help you master your weapons and begin building like a pro. From close-quarters combat to surviving the final ten, get ready for an action-packed adventure!

ARE YOU AN ULTIMATE
FORTNITE FAN?

Want to show off how much of a fearless Fortnite expert
you are? See how many of these are true for you...

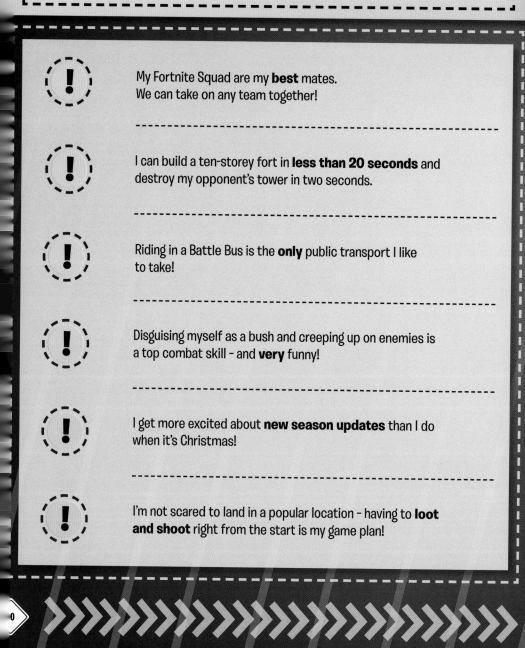

(!) My Fortnite Squad are my **best** mates.
We can take on any team together!

(!) I can build a ten-storey fort in **less than 20 seconds** and
destroy my opponent's tower in two seconds.

(!) Riding in a Battle Bus is the **only** public transport I like
to take!

(!) Disguising myself as a bush and creeping up on enemies is
a top combat skill - and **very** funny!

(!) I get more excited about **new season updates** than I do
when it's Christmas!

(!) I'm not scared to land in a popular location - having to **loot
and shoot** right from the start is my game plan!

I wish **V-Bucks** were actually real money - paying for stuff in shops with **V-Bucks** would be sick!

I know what **SMG**, **RPG** and **PVP** mean - I basically only talk in Fortnite initials and slang!

I'm an **ultra-accurate shot** and can take down long-range targets with my eyes closed!*

I'm reading this bangin' Battle Royale guidebook, so I must be a Fortnite **legend**!

When I walk past a tree in real life, I try to swing at it to collect wood. **Epic fail!**

I love pulling out **epic Emotes** from Fortnite - the Floss, Electro Shuffle, Jubilation and Dab dances are no problem!

*Okay, if I actually closed my eyes I'd probably never hit **anything**, but you know what I mean.

FAST FACTS AND SICK STATS

All the numbers you need to know about the most amazing video game on the planet!

60

There are over **60** weapons and explosives in Battle Royale, from pistols to shotguns and rifles. These range from Common (grey) to Legendary (orange) in rarity.

34,000,000

Battle Royale is HUGE on streaming sites and YouTube. The official Fortnite Twitch channel boasts more than **34 million** views, and on YouTube over **4 million** subscribers check out their awesome videos.

4,000,000

200

The minigun, compact SMG, SMG and double barrel shotgun all reach a DPS of over **200**. Get your hands on these and the enemy's going down, dude!

It's estimated that the pro Fortnite stars can make as many as **200 actions** per minute in close combat survival. Their fingertips must be on fire!

20,000,000

The biggest and best Fortnite YouTuber is Tyler 'Ninja' Blevins. This pro gamer has clocked up **20 million** YouTube subs, over **475 million** Twitch views, and has **4.5 million** Twitter followers!

475,000,000

4,500,000

Up to **80 million** players join a Battle Royale game each month! The game came to **Android** and **Nintendo Switch** in 2018, which helped player numbers to rocket.

80,000,000

200

Fortnite has an in-game currency, called V-Bucks, but it's free to play. V-Bucks can be acquired by spending real money, and items like **Emotes** and **skins** usually cost between **200** and **1,500** in the store.

1,500

$100,000,000

Fortnite has become an instant hit in the eSports competitive gaming world. Epic Games handed out an eye-popping **$100 million** prize pool for the first year of competition. Ker-ching!

TAKE A SHOT

To be a pro player you've got to understand all the key combat controls AND what's being shown on your screen.

Take Control

To become an elite Fortnite fighter, you might have to spend some cash on a **console control pad** just like the streaming stars use. Gaming company Scuf make top-level controllers with high-performance grips and **programmable back panels**, keeping your fingers free to do more damage.

Play Time

If you're not sure of a certain controller setting or button function, use the **Playground game mode** to practise using it. In Playground, you and your team have the island to yourselves, and you can spend **ages** trying new settings, weapons or items without being knocked by an enemy.

Quick Fix

In console settings, having the **auto sort consumables to right** option enabled is a winning move. This automatically keeps any **healing items** (like med kits and shields) to the right of your inventory, allowing quicker access to weapons. Most pros also opt to have **aim assist** switched on to boost shooting accuracy.

Crucial Countdown

The best Battle Royale gamers are not bothered by the in-game kills count, which is shown by the figure next to the skull inside a black circle. Instead, they concentrate on the **number of players** still left in the battle and also on the storm countdown clock. Fortnite is about **surviving, not killing**!

Keyboard King

If you're a PC player and you want to fire your Fortnite success rate up a notch, **try rebinding your keys.** Instead of using the default key controls for weapons and builds, you can rebind (reset) them in the input tab in the settings cog. Having a set of keys that you prefer for **building** is especially helpful.

VITAL SIGNS

You've got to keep a close eye on these important screen signs and details when you're deep in a Fortnite fight.

Keep Watch

Your ammo status is **vital**. Don't waste bullets, and always watch your **remaining ammo figure.** This is the number on the right.

24 | 34

Poorly Pals

In Duos and Squads, your teammates' health and shield is shown in the top left. Keep track on how well your pals are, and try to **help them** if they're suffering.

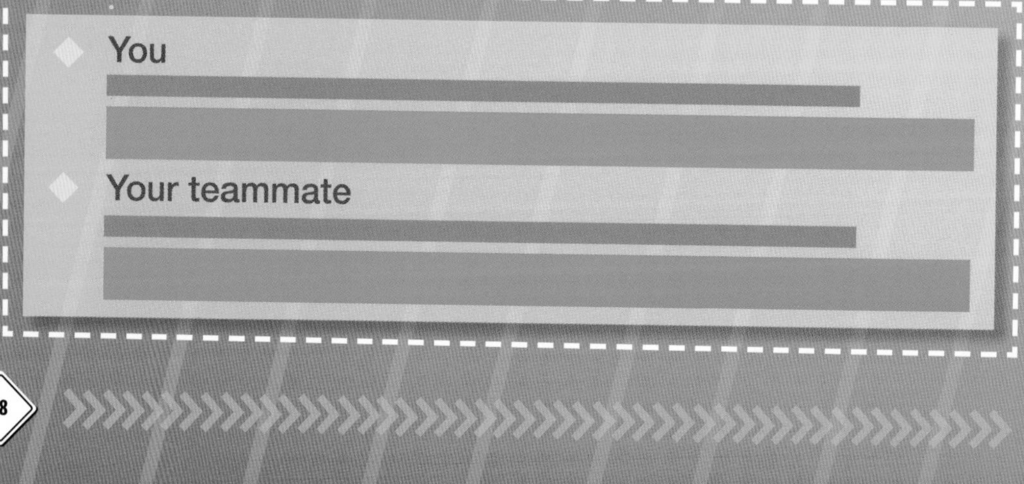

◆ You

◆ Your teammate

Bullseye

Aim for this dot with your **pickaxe** when you're bashing trees and items for mats. It's the **quickest** way to collect and harvest.

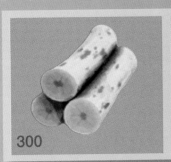

Over Here

In the pre-game lobby area, look out for an exclamation mark appearing by your item shop or locker tab. It means there's something **new** there or something you need to do.

Stocked Up

This shows how much **wood, brick** and **metal** you've farmed. Try to keep all above **300** if you can.

300   300   300

Next Level

If you're feeling brave, go to **HUD** in game settings and **turn the visuals off**. You'll be playing with no map or health bars - ultra tricky!

FORTNITE PHRASES

If you're a top-level gamer you'll need to know these words and expressions...

Rez

Teammates can **rez** (resurrect or revive) a **knocked** pal by using their healing items to boost that player's health.

Nerfed

Game developer Epic often **nerfs** a weapon or function, which means they reduce its **power** or **effectiveness**.

Buffed

The opposite of **nerfed**. Seeing your fave shotgun or explosive get an increase in power is awesome!

Knocked

If you take damage to your health or shield by the enemy, you've been **knocked**. This could lead to elimination.

GG

Meaning **'good game'**, Squad members often say this to each other at the end of a brilliant Battle Royale.

Mats

Wood, brick or **metal** materials are called this by serious Fortnite fighters. Harvesting mats is important in gameplay.

Lag

The annoying delay in Battle Royale caused by problems with your WiFi connection. No one loves **lag**!

Emote

Click the **Emote** button when you're on the island and watch your character dance, move and boogie like a hero!

Noob

A fun word called out when a new player is in the game. **Noobs** are often eliminated pretty quickly - sorry, dudes!

Tagged

When you get a hit on another player. For example you can **tag** the enemy for 50 damage, or whatever your weapon inflicts.

No-Skin

A player using the **default skin** in Fortnite. **'Noobs'** and **'No-Skins'** often mean the same thing.

OG

A word used to describe a Fortnite player who has been on the scene since the game started in **2017**.

Rush

You can be **rushed** by enemies or **rush** them, meaning to take a fast approach from the ground or up high.

Meta

A sick phrase used by serious gamers. It means **'most effective tactic available'**.

Vault

This happens in season updates when Epic removes weapons, items or functions from the game.

Shred

Dish out some serious damage to opponents, buildings and forts, and you'll be **shredding** them to pieces.

POI

This means **point of interest**, which is something that stands out on the map. The castle in Haunted Hills is a **POI**.

Beta

You may see this on loading screens. It means that a game **isn't finished** or fully developed by Epic yet.

Strat

Duos and Squads must know their **strat** (strategy) before landing from the **Battle Bus**.

Wingmen

The brave dudes who ride on the **X-4 Stormwing** wings when you're behind the controls.

TT

Gamers will shorten **Tomato Temple** and **Tilted Towers** to just **TT**. It can be confusing in Duos and Squads!

Combo

A combination of two or more things, such as a combo of weapons being used by a gamer to take down an enemy.

Ping

Similar to lag. It explains the time it takes for info from your server to travel to the Fortnite server and back again.

DPS

Meaning **Damage Per Second**. The bigger your weapon's **DPS**, the more dangerous you'll be!

MMO

An abbreviation of **massive multiplayer online game**. Fortnite is the biggest **MMO** in the gaming universe!

TTV

Some top gamers use **TTV** in their name tag, and it means that they stream on **Twitch**.

Teaming

In Solos, it's **against Fortnite rules** to 'team-up' with another solo player to defeat enemies.

Gear-up

Linked to **looting**, the best Fortnite pros can **gear-up** quickly and gather a good batch of weapons and shields early on.

PLAY SAFE, STAY SAFE

To play Fortnite Battle Royale, you'll compete against random players from around the world.

In Solos there will be 99 other gamers who you don't know. So if you're old enough to play, it's important to **keep yourself safe online** and follow these guidelines and tips.

Find Friends

You can Squad-up with people you know by sending friend requests. You may also receive friend requests. Never accept a request **if you do not know who that person is** directly. If it's a 'friend of a friend', ask your parent or guardian if it is okay to accept first.

Password Protection

As in any online game, always use **passwords that are strong** and very difficult for someone else to guess. Don't use your first name or surname as a password or as a username. A good tip is to make sure your parent or guardian also knows what both of these are.

Epic Fail

Epic, the people who make Fortnite, will never ask you to tell them your password. If you ever receive a message from someone asking you to reveal your password – even if they claim to be from Epic – never give it, and be sure to **inform an adult** straight away.

Speak Out

Some parents or guardians may not be sure what Fortnite actually is, so make sure that you **talk to them** about what the game is about and what happens on-screen. It's important to let your parents or guardians know when you're online and how long you have been playing.

Sounds Good

Most gamers use headphones and a microphone to chat with friends. If you also turn the **volume up** on your screen or monitor, the people around you at home can hear what's going on and feel assured that the gaming behaviour is **appropriate** for you.

Report It

Epic encourages any **bad behaviour** that happens during Battle Royale to be **reported** to them. This includes cheating, because they hate cheaters as much as you do! Go to the feedback icon, click on **player** and report the player's name and what happened.

Be Polite

Just like in everyday life, Fortnite players should **behave politely** and chat or message each other in a nice way. This is also known as **game etiquette**. Tell your parents or guardians if something happens which upsets you. Remember, we're all huge Fortnite fans and want to enjoy the game together!

Factor This

Epic has a function called **two-factor authentication (2FA)** which helps protect your account from unauthorized access. It means you need to enter an additional code when you sign in. You'll need to opt in to this in your account settings and follow the instructions.

Free V-Bucks

Some websites or YouTube channels offer to give you free V-Bucks. Be extremely careful about this as there's always a catch involved. The best advice is to ignore websites like this, or at the very least, never visit one unless an adult is supervising you.

BIGGEST BATTLE ROYALE
SHOCKS

With every update comes a few surprising new-season shocks. Take a look at some of the biggest game changes in Fortnite history!

FORTNITE FACT!

The map's landmass actually extended further into the sea with this **snowy shock** in season seven.

What's the shock? Ice and snow covers the south-west of the map.

When? Season seven

Fortnite became a winter wonderland when **freezing terrain** took over **Flush Factory** and **Greasy Grove**. **Frosty Flights, Polar Peak** and **Happy Hamlet** all emerged from the ice! Check it out in much more detail on **page 126**. There was a Christmassy touch too, with the ability to wrap weapons and vehicles as part of the battle pass.

What's the shock? Floating island appears over Loot Lake.

When? Season six

If you thought **Loot Lake** was dull, the stakes were literally raised in season six when the **floating island** took to the skies above it! Players simply had to step into the **whirlpool** on the ground to be thrown up into the sky and have their glider deployed. The island moved around and pros soon used it to help cover the map quickly with their glider open.

What's the shock? A meteor crashes into the map and blasts Dusty Depot.

When? Season four

The impact had been expected for a while, but in season four a **mighty meteor** (or a comet as some called it!) smashed the surface. It turned **Dusty Depot** into **Dusty Divot** and a new battle zone was created. Fragments of the meteor, known as **hop rocks**, scattered the ground and allowed players to jump high into the air!

What's the shock? 50v50 mode where every weapon is of Legendary variety.

When? Season five

Known as **50v50** Solid Gold, this mega **Limited Time Mode** was totally bonkers! Two giant teams battled it out and every weapon had Legendary power, which meant **rifles, shotguns** and **machine guns** were maxed out. The enemy's Battle Bus had a red outline and battle lines were marked on the map - players crossed them at their own risk!

THE STORM
STUFF YOU NEED TO KNOW!

Staying in the storm's safe zone is crucial
in Battle Royale. Take in these stats and tips
to help you ride the storm like a pro.

! FORTNITE FACT!

In season five the **storm wall**
could destroy structures in the last
few circles, but Epic removed this
function **just a few weeks later**.

The first four safe zones do not move. Then, from **storm circle** five to nine, the centre shrinks to somewhere away from the existing safe zone. **Always keep track of where it's moving to**.

The wait time and the shrink time are **two different things**. The first (blue clock) counts down the time that the safe zone has in its current size and location. The shrink time (the cloud in purple circle) shows **how long** it will be reducing for.

In the seventh, eighth and ninth **storm circle** there is no wait time. Now the circle just keeps on shrinking as the endgame approaches.

Once the **Battle Bus** has moved across the island, players only have one minute until the first **storm circle** shows up.

Gamers take **maximum storm damage** in the final four **storm circle** phases. At this time it'll zap ten health per second. In the first two phases you're only hit for one health per second.

Noobs often hang out by the edge of the storm as they try to stay away from top-level gamers. So spending some time there can **quickly boost your kill count**.

It seems so obvious, but running in a straight line is the quickest way to reach the safe zone! **Zigzag** or **diagonal** running is much slower and you could suffer storm damage because of it.

SAVE THE WORLD

You may be a class Battle Royale gamer, but what do you know
about the other Fortnite game called Save The World?
Here's your 60-second guide...

Monster Mission

Solo players, or teams of up to four, take on missions and battle monsters known as **Husks**.

Get Crafty

Like in **Battle Royale**, crafting and building is a big part of the game. Your structures can defend locations and you'll need **schematics** (plans) to help you construct.

Shelter

You have a **storm shield**, which is a permanent base that you build. Heroes venture from the **storm shield** to defeat monsters and rescue survivors.

Hero Types

Gamers take on missions as one of four main types of heroes. These are **Soldier**, **Constructor**, **Outlander** and **Ninja**. Each has their own skills and strengths.

Wreak Havoc

Husks usually inflict damage with **melee attacks** and use their hands to cause chaos. Watch out for **Pitchers** - they'll throw bones and team up to hurt you!

Squad Goals

The missions set for your Squad include delivering the bomb, fighting the storm and retrieving data. You'll also have 20 minutes to find **six survivors** - it's a scary and tough task!

Winning Weapons

Similar to **Battle Royale**, there are different weapons to help you. **Soldiers** are the perfect match for firing **rifles** and **pistols**. Your trusty **axe** is used for harvesting and smashing **Husks** in close combat.

BATTLE ROYALE ROUND-UP

You know your way around Fortnite, you can drop onto the map like a pro, and looting and shooting is easy stuff! Time to recap on your skills so far...

- Top-level knowledge of the controls and making in-game decisions quickly.

- Ability to select a weapon, fire accurately and switch to another one.

- Understanding what words, phrases and sayings mean in Fortnite.

- Staying safe online and knowing the rules and how to behave.

- Recognising that Fortnite is the biggest game ever and that it will never stop being awesome!

FORTNITE WEAPONS:
EXPERT GUIDE

To blast yourself into the endgame, a detailed knowledge of weapons is essential. Heroes need to know the strengths, weaknesses and tactics for using each firearm on the island. From shotguns to assault rifles, grenades to snipers, you're about to discover all of the info a pro gamer needs.

CLOSE-RANGE WEAPONS

Elite players practise short-range battles for hours, making sure that they are comfortable operating the best weapons in close-up duels. Check out the vital info on five firearms that can get the job done!

Pump shotgun

Rarity: Uncommon and Rare
DPS: 70
Damage: 100
Fire rate: 0.7
Reload time: 4.6 seconds
Magazine size: 5

FORTNITE FACT!

Some gamers think the **'double pump'** glitch of switching between two pump **shotguns** and firing multiple shots is cheating, and should never have been allowed!

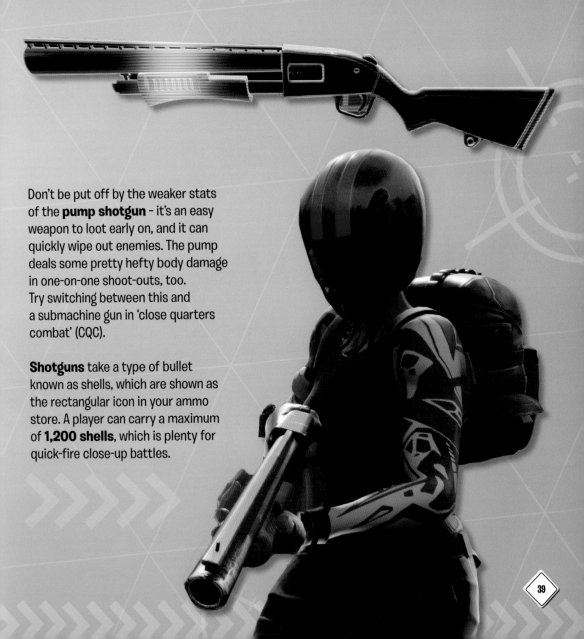

Don't be put off by the weaker stats of the **pump shotgun** - it's an easy weapon to loot early on, and it can quickly wipe out enemies. The pump deals some pretty hefty body damage in one-on-one shoot-outs, too. Try switching between this and a submachine gun in 'close quarters combat' (CQC).

Shotguns take a type of bullet known as shells, which are shown as the rectangular icon in your ammo store. A player can carry a maximum of **1,200 shells**, which is plenty for quick-fire close-up battles.

Tactical shotgun

Rarity: Common, Uncommon, Rare, Legendary and Epic

DPS: 130.5

Damage: 87

Fire rate: 5.1

Reload time: 5.7 seconds

Magazine size: 8

Don't avoid picking up the **tactical shotgun** if it appears when you loot - this weapon is still a brute! The main advantage it has over the pump and heavy is its larger magazine size. The tactical cracks out eight when the other pair are five and seven respectively.

The Rare version's about half a second quicker to reload than the Common and has seven more damage and 10.5 DPS. Its speedy fire rate will see a couple of taps on the trigger inflict serious close-up damage, but watch out for the slow reload time.

Heavy shotgun

Rarity: Legendary and Epic

DPS: 77

Damage: 77

Fire rate: 1.0

Reload time: 5.6 seconds

Magazine size: 7

When the enemy is so close that you can smell their sweat, **shotguns** are what you need to take them down! Many pro gamers will switch to the **heavy shotgun** in **CQC** because of its large mag size. You also don't need amazing accuracy with this fearsome firearm.

Like all shotgun weapons, a player with maximum health still won't be wiped out with a single blast to the head from this gun. But with the heavy's 192.5 headshot damage, a quick body pump afterwards will do the business. See ya!

Submachine gun

- - - - - - - - - - - - - -

Rarity: Common, Uncommon and Rare

DPS: 228

Damage: 19

Fire rate: 12

Reload time: 2.2 seconds

Magazine size: 30

At close- to medium-range, not many opponents can live with the power of the **submachine gun**. With a huge DPS in all three rarities, as well as a phenomenal fire rate, it packs the power to blow enemies away as you reach the **final ten**!

Avoid using it to take down buildings as the sub's structure damage is **too weak**. It's an accurate weapon and has the advantage of being quiet, too! Blast some bullets with this and only players close by will be alerted to your fire.

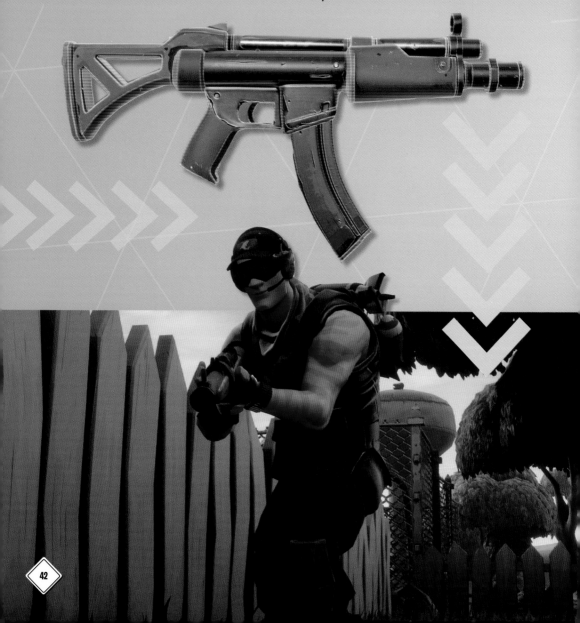

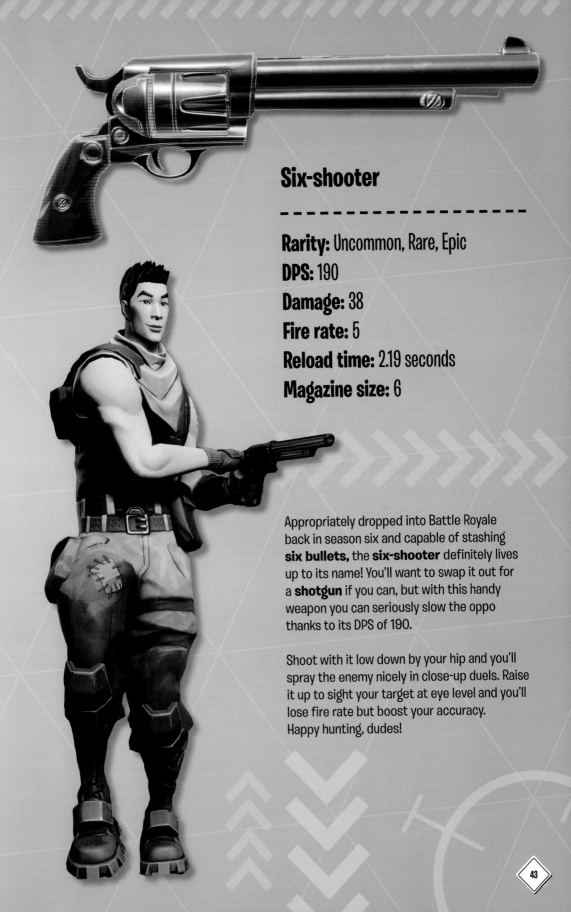

Six-shooter

Rarity: Uncommon, Rare, Epic

DPS: 190

Damage: 38

Fire rate: 5

Reload time: 2.19 seconds

Magazine size: 6

Appropriately dropped into Battle Royale back in season six and capable of stashing **six bullets,** the **six-shooter** definitely lives up to its name! You'll want to swap it out for a **shotgun** if you can, but with this handy weapon you can seriously slow the oppo thanks to its DPS of 190.

Shoot with it low down by your hip and you'll spray the enemy nicely in close-up duels. Raise it up to sight your target at eye level and you'll lose fire rate but boost your accuracy. Happy hunting, dudes!

MID-RANGE WEAPONS

Sometimes getting close to your enemy can be the wrong move and you'll need to fire accurately from a safer distance. Assault rifles should be your go-to weapon for this, and these bad boys are the pick of the bunch!

Thermal scoped assault rifle

- - - - - - - - - - - - - - - - - - -

Rarity: Legendary and Epic

DPS: 64.8

Damage: 36

Fire rate: 1.8

Reload time: 2.185 seconds

Magazine size: 15

If you enjoy medium-range duels with the **scoped rifle**, the thermal version is very similar – but with a few fancy tricks to pull out! Use its scope to detect heat signatures from Supply Drops, chests and even enemy players. These will **glow yellow** when detected.

The **thermal scoped** is a highly accurate rifle but it does carry significant recoil, so you'll need to tap-fire this semi-auto piece of kit. It's also great for hunting down the opposition from a distance, as you can scan the horizon for shooting targets. Epic and Legendary versions are very similar to each other.

Burst assault rifle

Rarity: Common, Uncommon, Rare, Legendary and Epic

DPS: 133.98

Damage: 33

Fire rate: 1.75

Reload time: 2.3 seconds

Magazine size: 30

It's a close call between the **SCAR** and the **burst rifle**, which is often called the **FAMAS** after the famous French firearm. It releases rounds in bursts of three, and has a greater accuracy because of it. Even the grey Common version is worth picking up if it's the only option you have when looting.

It's worth noting that the **burst assault** blasts out a much higher structure damage than other rifles, even the **heavy shotgun**. It can be used to crack wooden defences and shred any oppo hiding away!

Assault rifle SCAR

Rarity: Legendary and Epic
DPS: 198
Damage: 36
Fire rate: 5.5
Reload time: 2.1 seconds
Magazine size: 30

With the Legendary **SCAR** stashed in your inventory, you'll feel ready for Battle Royale dominance. **Assault rifles** pump out a high rate of medium bullets and can even be used for long distance firing if needed. Short and sharp bursts are best at medium range, and avoid **spraying and praying** in combat.

The suppressed assault rifle **SCAR** was dropped in during season five and quickly became a fave. It only dips 16.5 behind the assault rifle **SCAR's** DPS, and with a silenced shot and almost laser-guided precision, opponents can be whacked in an instant!

Heavy assault rifle

Rarity: Rare, Epic and Legendary

DPS: 157.5

Damage: 42

Fire rate: 3.75

Reload time: 2.52 seconds

Magazine size: 25

The first heavy weapon to come with a Rare version, this **assault rifle** does a fab job of taking down players at a distance. Even though it's not as dangerous as most other rifles, if the heavy's by your side you'll stand a chance of being the last fighter standing!

Using medium bullets, take a split second to sight your opponent and use light taps on the trigger to keep an accurate shot. Usually your target will take too much damage to be able to react, giving you a vital window to wipe out their health and shield. Good work!

Minigun

- - - - - - - - - - - - - - - - - -

Rarity: Epic and Legendary

DPS: 252

Damage: 21

Fire rate: 12

Reload time: zero

Magazine size: n/a

You'll find more details about the **minigun** on **page 62**, but there's no way it could be left off this list of lethal mid-range guns! Don't worry too much about the differences between purple and the more sought-after orange, as the DPS and structure damage are very similar.

As well as looking mega mean with its **six-shooter** design, players must grab a top handle to keep the **minigun** steady when firing. If you're not a very accurate shot from distance, have a blast on this and see the carnage you'll create!

LONG-RANGE WEAPONS

Sniper rifles are the must-have machine when you're talking about deadly hits from a distance. Take your time to perfect these weapons and you'll see your kill count rise in tense top ten shoot-outs. Don't miss the important RPG info on page 54, either!

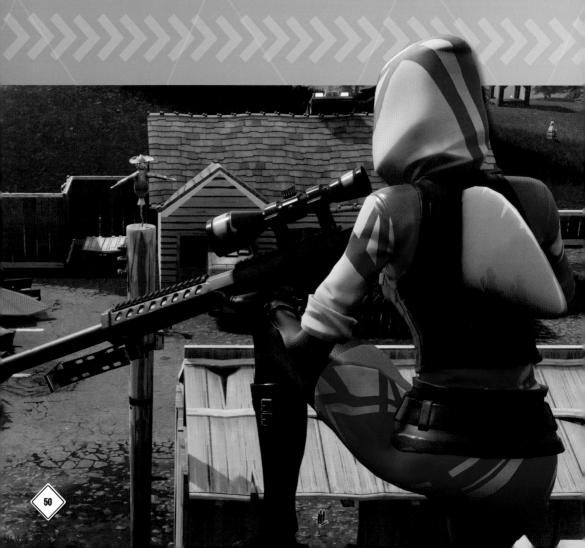

Semi-auto sniper rifle

- - - - - - - - - - - - - - - - -

Rarity: Rare

DPS: 93.6

Damage: 78

Fire rate: 1.2

Reload time: 2.5 seconds

Magazine size: 10

If the reload time and single-bullet mag size of the bolt-action gets on your nerves, look to loot the **semi-auto sniper** instead. It's quite evenly matched in green and blue versions and two precise headshots will signal the end for your enemy!

The **semi-auto** boasts a much higher fire rate than the other two sniper rifles here, which means you can blast multiple shots to seriously confuse and wound whoever's in your range. You'll need to master the recoil to keep your targets tightly focused.

Bolt-action sniper rifle

Rarity: Epic

DPS: 36.3

Damage: 110

Fire rate: 0.33

Reload time: 2.8 seconds

Magazine size: 1

Your best chance to loot one of these beauties is from a supply drop. If it does appear, then scramble like crazy to collect it! **The bolt-action** is incredible from a distance, offering a double dose of power and precision that can eliminate opponents with ease. Its structural damage of 110 makes it even more of a beast.

Check this out! The **bolt's** headshot power is 275 (Epic), which means it'll destroy an enemy player with full health and shield. Wow! It needs reloading after each heavy bullet used though, so mix it up with a **quick-loading** weapon.

Hunting rifle

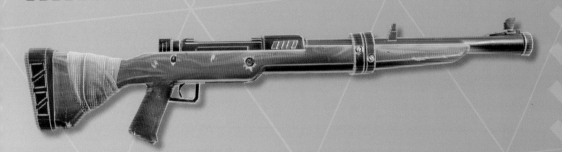

Rarity: Rare and Uncommon

DPS: 72

Damage: 90

Fire rate: 0.8

Reload time: 1.8 seconds

Magazine size: 1

Another wonderful one-shot weapon that's wicked in warfare! Its lack of a scope to sight opponents gives you a wider view of what's around you, but it is possible to zoom in slightly. The **hunting rifle** does a decent job in medium-range shoot-outs, too.

Rocket Launcher

Rarity: Epic and legendary

DPS: 90.75

Damage: 121

Fire rate: 0.75

Reload time: 3.24 seconds

Magazine size: 1

As you'll discover on other pages, the **rocket launcher** is a vital tool in taking down Solo players and Squads in epic end-game battles. Don't worry about having to loot the orange Legendary **RPG,** as this epic model is only a tiny bit less powerful.

The **rocket launcher's** reload time may look like a weakness, but the sheer devastation it causes gives your oppo little time to strike back. Load up another rocket and fire away again – just in case the first launch didn't finish off the enemy!

In October 2017, Epic realized the RPG's power was just a little too much. They had to increase its reload time by **20 per cent** to make shoot-outs fairer! Elite gamers didn't make a fuss though - they just increased their deadly accuracy with the **RPG** on their shoulder.

The mind-blowing guided missile was first dropped into Battle Royale in season three, taking a short vault break in season six. Technically it's an explosive weapon, but it's one of the best long-distance destroyers ever to appear in the game. In Epic and Legendary, it kicks out 400 structure damage, and is controlled remotely by the user.

FORTNITE FACT!

The **RPG** and **guided missile** can be ridden by your teammates, but you'll need a lot of practice in **Playground** mode to master this move like the pros.

EXPLOSIVES AND GRENADES

Rifles and shotguns rule in combat, but players also need an explosive edge entering the endgame!

Know Your 'Nades

There are a few types of explosive **grenades**, and Epic love to unleash different versions in new seasons. At 105, the **Common grenade** packs the most damage, and structurally it'll zap 375. Players can be tooled up with a max of ten. **Grenades** have a short throw distance, but chuck one at your camped-out enemy to blow their cover so that you can rush in and ambush.

Bouncing Back

Grenade launchers come in Rare, Epic and Legendary. Don't sweat too much about finding the orange one though, as there's just ten DPS difference between the three. This **explosive rocket weapon** wreaks havoc in a tense top ten tussle, but here's a warning: avoid firing too close to structures or hills as it can **bounce back** and damage you!

Stinky Stuff

Wanna get up the nose of your Battle Royale foes? Detonate a **stink bomb** close to them and drain ten damage every second for nine seconds. It's a great Duo or Squad tactic and allows your teammates to plan a group attack while the enemy **smells the pain**. Just make sure the thrower avoids the gruesome gas or they'll take damage, too!

Deadly Damage

Only use explosives on targets that are a **good distance away** from you. If you ignore this advice, you could suffer serious blast damage yourself (but fortunately your teammates won't!). If your pals **ride rockets** that you've fired, they must jump off at the right point to avoid taking a hit as well.

Lethal Launchers

Stick the Legendary season six **quad launcher** on your shoulder and reel off one, two, three or four rockets to totally take down towers! The **quad's** fast firing rate stuns whoever's unlucky enough to be in the way. The **guided missile** has been vaulted a few times to tweak its stunning power. Whenever it's in play, it's a game-changing rocket in the final ten and it's as effective as the **RPG**.

Rocket Reminder

Rockets can cause panic and mayhem in your enemy's mind. But remember, they travel quite slowly and it's often easy to detect where they are fired from. This could give away your location at a crucial stage in the battle and lead to your elimination.

FORTNITE WEAPONS:
EXTRA ESSENTIALS

Max out your pro weapon skills and shred the enemy with these tips and tactics.

Even pro gamers who need a calculator to count their Victory Royales make use of the simple **damage trap**. Noobs frequently fall into the trap of entering a building primed with a spiky tile that springs to inflict 150 damage. In the final ten, placing traps on ceilings is the perfect way to **strike and spike**. What a nasty surprise!

Pro gamers loved making use of the crazy **chiller trap** introduced in season six. Lay this ice-cool item down and it'll send your enemies slipping and sliding. Use it on your ramps and watch the **frantic frozen footwork**!

The **compact SMG** is a tasty tool to have at your disposal. In short-range combat, you can shoot from the hip without needing to be massively accurate. This baby fires off 40 rounds in one go! Make sure that you begin reloading at the right time though, or you could leave yourself open to critical hits. Watch the light bullet counter.

Had a blast on the Epic or Legendary **heavy sniper rifle** yet? It's an utterly unreal weapon, taking 150/157 damage to players and a mind-boggling 1,050/1,100 to buildings. In the final ten, forts and towers don't stand a chance against this. In fact, not much is left standing after this has been unleashed!

The best gamers base their combat style and approach on the **weapons in their inventory**, or those that they feel most confident with. **Shotguns** and **SMGs** are ideal for an aggressive gamer who revels in **CQC**. If **rifles** and **snipers** are your thing, you're more passive so keep your distance and a low profile.

To eliminate the reload waiting time with your weapon, loot the monster **minigun**. It will fire light bullets until you completely run out, with a fire rate of 12 and DPS of 216 or 228. Remember that is has a short delay after first letting rip, so it's vital to surprise the enemy.

Don't forget to use the **guided missile weapon** as a super scouting tool, too. Blast it and follow the missile's path to see what's around you as you prepare for battle on the ground. It's a strong weapon, but a great **tracking device** on the opposition.

Some Fortnite fans said that the introduction of the **grappler** in September 2018 was a bit like being Spider-Man on the island! It's not a weapon, but fire the **grappler** and it'll attach to a structure to pull and swing you along. It can be used ten times before depleting and is a **top tactic** to swoop in on your opponent before unleashing a weapon.

WHICH WEAPON
WOULD YOU USE?

Now that you've studied all the sick Battle Royale weapons, decide which one you would use in each of these crucial combat shoot-outs.

1 You're about 15 metres away from your Solo enemy in open grassland. The opposition is jumping around to make it harder for you to land a hit.

Which weapon's best?

Heavy shotgun   Suppressed pistol   Hunting rifle

2

You're perched on a high building, looking down on a mid-range target that is moving slowly through a field.

Which weapon's best?

Submachine gun   Bolt-action sniper rifle   Hand cannon

3

You've discovered that the enemy is hiding in a defensive fort in the far distance and doesn't know that you're about to strike.

Which weapon's best?

Heavy sniper rifle   Grenade launcher   Rocket launcher

EXPERT ADVICE:

1 The **heavy shotgun** is perfect in close-range shooting, even when targets don't stay still.

2 The **bolt-action** is brilliant for blasting the enemy with a single, powerful shot from mid- to long-distance range.

3 The **rocket launche**r only needs to be pointed at the target and it'll fly straight into the structure and inflict huge damage.

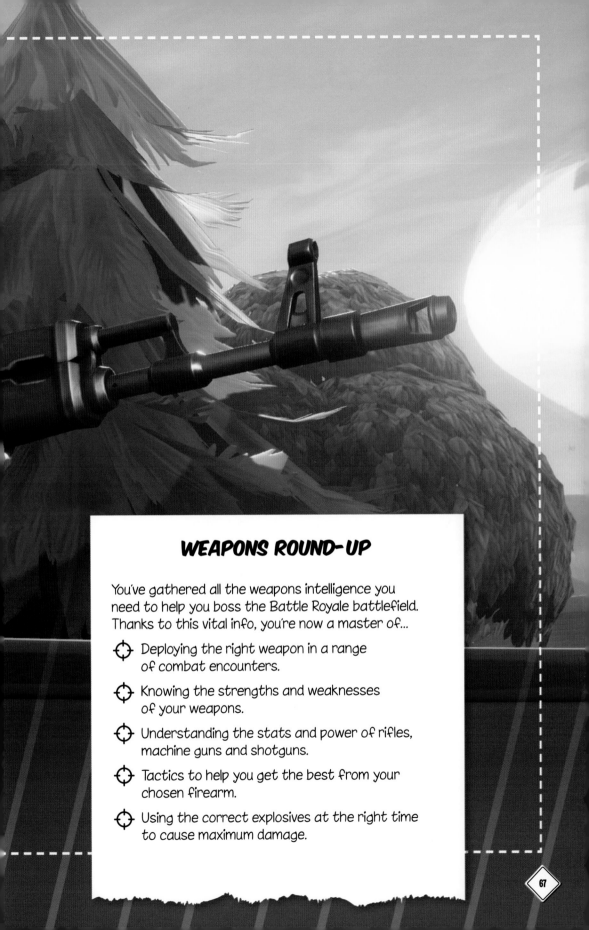

WEAPONS ROUND-UP

You've gathered all the weapons intelligence you need to help you boss the Battle Royale battlefield. Thanks to this vital info, you're now a master of...

- Deploying the right weapon in a range of combat encounters.

- Knowing the strengths and weaknesses of your weapons.

- Understanding the stats and power of rifles, machine guns and shotguns.

- Tactics to help you get the best from your chosen firearm.

- Using the correct explosives at the right time to cause maximum damage.

BECOME AN ACE
BUILDER

There's no escaping it - Battle Royale is as much about building and creating as it is shooting and sniping! Top-level fighters can knock up a defensive fort or a vital vantage point in a matter of seconds. Turn over to discover the key points and crucial tips to max out your building game and take your gameplay to a higher level.

HARVESTING

WITH THE BEST OF 'EM

Gamers can't build anything unless they gather materials after landing. These top tips will help you harvest like a legend.

Wood is Good

Make collecting **wood** your priority in the early part of games. Don't fuss over harvesting **metal** or **brick** at this stage, as the storm is constantly moving and you'll be leaving structures behind. **Wood** should be good enough to defeat and defend against noobs.

Tree-mendous Tactic

When using your **axe** to harvest a tree for **wood**, it's often a good idea not to destroy it completely. If it does disappear you'll be left without something to hide behind if you come under a surprise attack. Leave the tree when it has a low health.

Pallets are Perfect

In the early scramble for mats, search out **wooden pallets**. These are often stacked by fences or stashed in towns and cities. Striking **pallets** is the best method to harvest wood for each hit. The least efficient are small wooden fences and gates.

Inspect Chests

Remember that **chests** have materials as well, and not just weapons and healing items. If it's too risky to harvest in the open, search for **chests** in buildings and gather **vital supplies** that way.

Deadly Move

The quickest way to **harvest** a big bunch of materials is to eliminate an opponent, then run over and gobble up their **dropped items**. Make sure it's safe to do so first and don't leave yourself open to a sniper bullet.

BECOME A
BUILDER PRO

Get to grips with the Builder Pro console mode
and see why it could be the best option for you.

! FORTNITE FACT!

The best **pro gamers** always
check and adjust their controller
sensitivity settings through
the cog icon tab.

What's the Difference?

Console players can choose to configure
their controller to **Builder Pro** or **Combat
Pro**. Builder Pro is designed to allow Xbox
or PS gamers to build almost as quickly
as PC users, but Fortnite fans are divided
on the good and bad points of each. Go to
the **settings** tab and select **controller**
to see the layout of both.

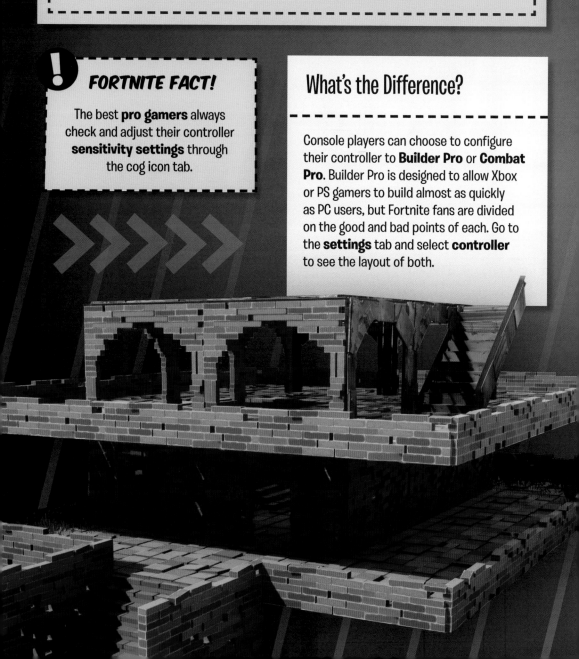

Spam's the Plan

In Builder Pro on console, don't be afraid to keep your finger pressed down and keep knocking up instant **walls** and **ramps**. The left trigger or **L2** (stairs), and right trigger or **R2** (walls), should become part of your muscle memory and a move that you can pull off without thinking!

Practice Makes Perfect

Elite Fortnite players have mastered Builder Pro, but they only achieved this through many hours of practice. Drop into **Playground** or **50vs50**, as it gives you a chance to farm lots of mats and begin getting used to this building set-up. Stick with it and your structures and creations will appear ultra quickly.

Ramp it Up

When it was introduced in season three, **Builder Pro** was quite revolutionary! You could put a ramp up before a wall, reaching the high ground quicker and taking control over an opponent during a battle situation. If your combat style is builder-fighter, you'll love it.

Spin to Win

Top-level builders will lay down stairs and ramps, then **spin** left or right to build walls and create a fort. Work out whether you're more comfortable **spinning** to the left or right (it makes no difference!) and practise until this becomes a natural move. **Spinning** quickly is a must when you're **panic building** to protect yourself.

Turbo Time

In the game control options, the pros never turn the **turbo building** function off. This option, combined with Builder Pro, allows bases, ramps and floors to spring up in a matter of seconds. It's a great tool for letting you cross water or get up steep hills fast!

Combat Test!

In Squads or Duos, stand next to a teammate in a safe zone on the map. One of you should be in **Builder Pro** and the other in **Combat Pro**. Begin ramp-wall pushing and see who builds the quickest - it's a smart way to see how each mode works, and if there's a big difference in speed!

PRO BUILDING
POWERRR!

The next six pages reveal building techniques and tips that will help you to become the best of the best...

!

FORTNITE FACT!

With 400HP, **metal** can survive strikes from Rare and Epic **grenades** and **rocket launchers**.

When you're building upwards, creating a **double ramp structure** will increase your chance of survival and of striking your opponent. The double width gives you more shelter from bullets, plus **the enemy won't know which side you'll begin shooting from**. If one side of your ramp is shot down, you'll still have the other side left.

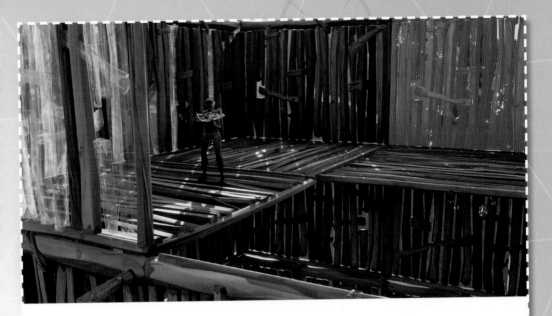

Don't create buildings that are **neat, tidy and predictable**. Instead, adopt an unpredictable and confusing build style. Try placing random walls and ramps inside your constructions that will **baffle enemies** when they attack from inside. This also helps you lay down traps in random places that can catch and crush them!

Never underestimate the power of wood, especially when you're panic building for protection. Of all the three materials, wood spawns the quickest and has the highest base health upon being placed down. Wood is also in abundance throughout the map, which means that reaching the 999 mats maximum is achievable for the best Fortniters!

To cap off a strong **defensive fort**, place **wooden roof structures** (pyramids) to completely surround the top level of your building. This gives you awesome protection from **bullets** and **grenades** in the mid-game or final phase, but you're also able to poke between the structures to spy on the enemy below.

If you're under fire from the ground and you know where the enemy is firing from or hiding, try building a **ramp** in their direction. It may sound strange, but a quickly created **ramp** straight towards your target gives you cover and a high spot to shoot from and eliminate the oppo. It's risky, but it can be very rewarding!

Building is **essential** in making the final ten and clinching victory, but it's also a handy way to stay away from the storm as it shrinks. Running through open fields or going up and down hills is tough and slow, so switch to **build mode** and knock up a **bridge** or a **ramp** to reach the safe zone much quicker!

Building is noisy and it can give away your **location** to nearby players. But if you spot the enemy near to you and see that they are building, take the opportunity to build too. The sound from the other player will mask what you're doing. It's a simple but smart tactic!

Expert Fortnite players will regularly **edit their buildings** to react to combat situations. For example, editing in a window provides a viewing point to the enemy and a sneaky sniper spot. Remember that editing an escape route via downwards ramps is a quick way to leave a building without having to jump outside and risk fall damage or being shot.

FORTNITE FACT!

You can fall from buildings of up to **three storeys** and not suffer damage. Any higher and you'll lose HP.

ESSENTIAL
BUILDING BASICS

It never hurts to be reminded of the simple steps that all builders need to remember. Learn these basics off by heart!

Ramps

It can be easy to forget, but internal things like **ramps** should be made from wood. It's quick to lay down and wood is easy to farm.

Brilliant Base

If you can, build **fort bases** from **metal** or **brick** as it'll be harder to destroy in the **final ten**.

Fort

Don't build complicated forts in the early or mid-game - you'll have to leave them as the storm moves.

Laying Traps

Treat **traps** like a form of building and creating. When you're making a fort, lay a **trap** near the base and enemy intruders could trigger it.

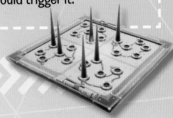

Look Out

Don't forget to add **windows** so that you have a **sniper point**.

Fierce Fights

Be prepared for **build fights,** which are short and sharp gun battles in the first storm circle. Here, the quickest builder usually wins!

BUILDING ROUND-UP

You've now got all the power and knowledge you need to become a master Fortnite builder! Time for a rundown of your pro building tips and secrets...

- Whether defending or attacking, you know the building designs that work.

- You're an expert harvester and you collect the mats that matter.

- You know different building styles and how to ramp up to victory.

- You know the HP and spawn rates of the three basic materials.

- You can edit a basic building to improve your chance of killing and surviving.

TAKE COMMAND OF
COMBAT

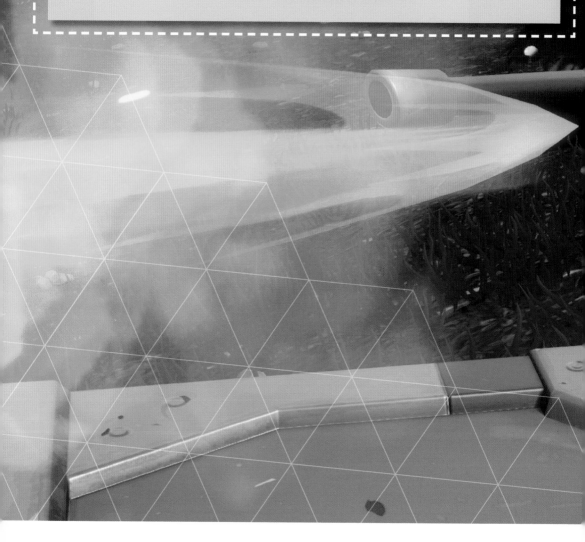

Flex your muscles and have weapons loaded - it's time to engage in enemy combat! The next 16 pages are packed with expert advice and tips to help you become the master of looting, shoot-outs, sniping and reaching the final phase. Covering Solos, Duos, Squads and top ten, take note and let the Battle Royale begin...

SOLO COMBAT
TACTICS AND TIPS

If it's you against the rest, these hints and helpful strategies will make you the battle boss!

Aim of the game

If you're not an expert aimer and struggle with your shooting accuracy, choose a weapon that has a higher DPS rating. For example, the tactical shotgun has nearly double the DPS of the pump shotgun.

Know the bus route

After you jump from the Battle Bus, you'll focus on landing and your first moves. Keep an eye on where the bus heads to, and anticipate which direction gamers will approach from on the map, plus any clusters of fighters. This can be a brain-busting tactic at first, but keep working at it!

Stand on opened doors

If you need to save mats, be super silent or cautious about entering a building through an opened door. Jump on top of the door and reach the first level that way. It's a simple Solo technique, but it could help you surprise the person inside.

Make an ambush

Solo fighters should look for the Legendary bush item and make the most of it. In open fields, you can stalk opponents under complete cover and make a quick-fire attack. Don't move too quickly though, and be sure to crouch down to blend in better.

Shield yourself

Solo gamers who end up going deep into a battle will usually be replenishing their shield more than their health. Always try to keep a shield potion in the healing slot of your inventory, because the shield will be reduced first if you're hit.

Smell spells trouble

With a stink bomb at the ready, you have a great item for one-on-one battles. It lasts for nine seconds and the cloud gives you time to move positions, approach the enemy, or snuff them out from a hiding spot.

Upper limit

Having the higher ground is a basic Battle Royale rule, but players often fail by rushing gamers above them without the proper weapons. Opponents up high can easily pick you off, so don't go there unless you have near-full health as well as plenty of rifle and SMG ammo.

DUO AND SQUAD
TACTICS AND TIPS

When you're part of
a team, deciding what your
tactics are and operating as
a well-organized group is key.

One Direction

Communicating with your team is vital for grabbing a group **Victory Royale**. Give the precise location of the enemy to the rest of your Squad by telling them the direction and numbers on your **compass** - don't just yell 'over there'! The **compass** shout-outs only work if your team is close together.

Inside Job

Grenade launchers do a top job of shredding forts, but perfecting the trajectory (path) of the fired 'nade is something that the pros work hard at. Looping the **grenade** so that it drops into an **enemy camp**, rather than just crashing a building's base, can inflict devastating health strikes on personnel.

Mini is Mighty

When hunting down Squads that hide out in towers and forts inside the final phase, try whipping out the **minigun** (if you have it in your arsenal). It's one of the best for destroying structures and it's a joy to be in charge of. Be sure to hold fire as soon as teammates storm in to loot.

Dream Team Move

Have you heard of **suppressive fire?** It's when a group sprays bullets together on a camped-out enemy, limiting their movements and allowing your pals to march in for a kill. The repeat firepower of the **semi-auto sniper rifle** is perfect for this tactic.

Good Call

Keep talking to your teammates and let them know what you need, especially healing items. For example, if you're an ace with **explosives** but don't have any, ask a team member to drop theirs so that you can pick it up and land a major strike for the team.

Crossbow

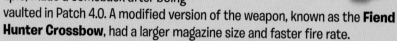

The **Crossbow** made its first appearance as part of Battle Royale's **Valentine's Day theme**, but it wasn't around for long. The famous Fortnite **Crossbow**, which comes in Rare and Epic, made a comeback after being vaulted in Patch 4.0. A modified version of the weapon, known as the **Fiend Hunter Crossbow**, had a larger magazine size and faster fire rate.

Mounted Turret

This awesome trap item in **Battle Royale** is Legendary! It's known as the **Mounted Turret** and has totally unlimited ammo. Fire it too much though, and it can overheat – you've been warned... It's also good to be aware that this item can be used by any player, no matter what team they're on. So, once you've got your mitts on a **Mounted Turret**, don't let it out of your sight. You can find **Mounted Turrets** in **Supply Drops**, **Vending Machines**, **Supply Llamas** and **floor loot**. Be sure to grab one when you get the chance!

10 TIPS IN THE FINAL TEN

If you're still struggling to clinch that vital Victory Royale, these tips and tactics will help make you the last one standing!

1 | If you are struck down in the **final ten**, don't sob and strop! Watch the rest of the battle and study the moves and tactics that the winner uses. What you see and learn will help you progress further in the future.

2

After eliminating an opponent when you're out in the open, **immediately** running for cover and sheltering to heal can be your best option. There could be up to eight others watching you and lining up a lethal shot!

3

In the endgame, master how to use the **rocket launcher** (RPG). In a fight with the final few players, it can wipe out a base with one shot and put you within touching distance of victory. A Legendary RPG dishes out 121 damage!

4 In your **equipment inventory**, order your weapons so that your top two guns are next to each other and you can quickly swap between them. Having your **assault rifle** next to your **shotgun** makes sense.

5 Always have **healing items** at the back of your inventory, and the weapons at the front. In combat you'll need to select a gun in double-quick time, but healing doesn't need to be quite so rapid.

6 In the final five or six, staying **close to the storm** can sometimes pay off. This tactic means that nothing can approach you from behind and the action is right there in front of you!

7 If you do take a hit, build cover **straight away** and don't waste valuable seconds looking to see who fired! Just speedily build a structure around you and then work out your next move.

8 Sprinting leaves a **dust trail** behind you that can be spotted from a distance and could give away your location. In the final ten, try **crouching** and **moving slowly** - it's quieter and won't alert other gamers.

9

To reach the endgame, you may need to play the short game first. Land in a popular location, like **Tilted Towers**, and perfect your shooting and combat moves. You may lose quickly and often, but you can restart in a minute or so.

10

Watch the pro YouTubers and streamers to see how they clinch Victory Royale **time and time again**. You'll pick up stacks of tips and have fun at the same time!

COMBAT ROUND-UP

Seeing off the 99 other players on the island is what Battle Royale is all about! Take a quick look back at the key combat skills and strengths that pro fighters need to have...

⊕ Deciding the best tactics to have from the Battle Bus and landing ready for action.

⊕ Mastering how to take down the enemy in Solos by looting quickly and knowing when to attack and defend your ground.

⊕ When playing in Duos and Squads, drawing on top teamwork powers and leading a group like a legend.

⊕ Inside the top ten, staying cool and clinical with weapons and explosives.

⊕ Being able to harvest and use med kits at the right time to keep you healthy in the endgame.

TAKE ON THE
TERRAIN

Battle Royale locations can be divided into six main types - suburbs, cities, farmland, desert, forest and ice biomes. Each has their own challenges and elite gamers have tons of tips and tactics to boss each terrain. Turn over to start your location guide...

SUBURBS

Get ready for close-range house-to-house combats in the suburbs of Pleasant Park and Retail Row. Grab a shotgun quickly!

The **suburbs** are busy, so watch out for attacks from any angle. Try to follow the tiny trail that a bullet leaves in the air to work out your attacker's location.

Use the **hills** and **high grounds** around the suburbs to scope out the enemy and plan the best tactic to attack.

There are lots of **buildings** in the suburbs. Use these to shelter and take on meds if your health has taken a hit.

FORTNITE FACT!

Using your **axe** to smash up a car will set off its alarm. You have been warned!

Crouch for a **sniping shot** behind a vehicle. Harvesting it for metal will be noisy, though.

There are fewer **open fields** in the suburbs, compared with farms, but there are still plenty of long-range engagements. As well as a **shotgun**, a **rifle** is always handy.

Top gamers always know their '**loot routes**' in the suburbs. These are the paths to take and locations to hit to discover **chests** and **loot.** This takes practice and a top memory!

Landing on the **rooftop** of a house could give your location away to enemies and make you too visible. In the suburbs, try looting from the ground floor up, or even start in the **basements** of buildings. Often **weapons** are located here.

It's best to stay away from **open areas** in the suburbs, like the sports field in Pleasant Park. You're too exposed to sniper bullets and there's nowhere to find instant cover if you come under attack.

Look out for cracked interior walls in suburban spots - there could be a **secret room** stashed with loot behind it! Break it down and take a look inside for helpful items and weapons that you'll need in the mid- to endgame.

Gamers are often tightly bunched together after landing in a popular suburb, such as **Retail Row** or **Lucky Landing**. Listen for the sounds of players harvesting cars or smashing through roofs, and approach them for a quick kill!

CITY SCENE

Tilted Towers first appeared on the map back in season two. It's rammed with high-rise buildings, houses and stores which makes it very popular in the early game.

Gathering resources and weapons in nearby **Snobby Shores**, then quickly going to **Tilted Towers** is a smart tactic.

Land even quicker by dropping onto the **top** of a building and looting from top to bottom.

FORTNITE FACT!

Tilted Towers is a central location and players there won't be caught by the storm in the early game.

After landing in a city, it can be a good tactic to loot key things, like **meds** and a **shotgun**, and then **hide out** for a little while. Let the hotheaded gamers blast each other early on, then venture out carefully into the city terrain.

Windows give a great spot to **zoom in** on the enemy and fire, but remember they can be a weakness too and leave you open to bullets. Fire a shot from a window, then duck back behind the wall by the window for protection.

Unless you enter **Tilted Towers** straight after leaving the Battle Bus, it's usually best to stay well away. Turning up later on at TT can be a big mistake, as the gamers there may already have good bases and hideouts.

- ⊕ Listen out for enemy footsteps, firing and harvesting.

- ⊕ Get the **high ground** in the city and pick off a few easy kills on players running through the streets.

- ⊕ Be prepared to panic build some shield walls if you're fired at in the streets.

- ⊕ Pull your parachute late on and land quickly into **Tilted Towers**.

Building-to-building combat is common in cities and towns. Many pro players focus on firing first without worrying too much about being accurate. A quick strike with a rifle will shock and surprise your city enemy!

Tilted Towers attracts a mix of gamers. Noobs could arrive because of the **huge loot** available, but experienced players like cities too, for the easy eliminations. It's difficult to guess the level of opponents you'll face!

FARMLAND

It's time to explore the barns and farmhouses of Fatal Fields.
Get ready to land and loot to discover the hidden chests!

A farm's barns are where **most loot and chests are hidden**. Explore them by either entering from the roof or the ground floor.

High ground further to the south is a strong **landing position**, but quickly head for barns and farmhouses in Fatal Fields.

FORTNITE FACT!

Some clever gamers used the scarecrow **stuffed skins** and **T-Pose Emote** to pretend to be scarecrows in Fatal Fields!

Avoid landing in the **centre** of the farmland in **Fatal Fields**. It's very open and you'll be spotted by other players. Without a weapon you could be picked off easily.

High **cornfields** are perfect for dodging a firefight or leaping out from to surprise someone.

If you see a big collection of **hay bales**, take a look behind as there's often a weapon stashed around them. Big piles of hay can be a clue that there's something sweet hiding in there!

Break down the **tall storage silos** to search for loot. Look underneath the bridge in shallow water, too.

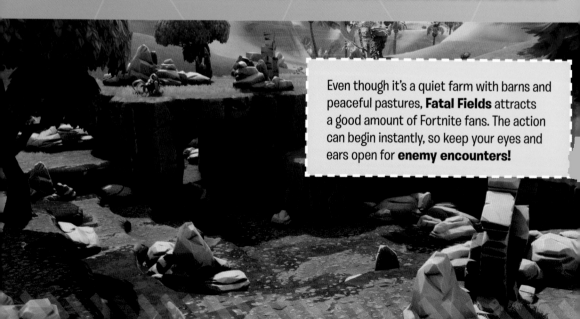

Even though it's a quiet farm with barns and peaceful pastures, **Fatal Fields** attracts a good amount of Fortnite fans. The action can begin instantly, so keep your eyes and ears open for **enemy encounters!**

Instead of looting every item you see on farmland, try leaving one or two. You can take a hiding position and then **pop out to blast** another player who rushes in to grab it!

There are some **cars** and **trucks** scattered around, which can be harvested for **metal**.

Visit the small **stone mines** to smash them up and stock up on resources.

DESERT

The first desert biome appeared in Paradise Palms.
It's hot, exciting, and full of battle action and looting.

FORTNITE FACT!

Paradise Palms replaced **Moisty Mire** on the map in season five.

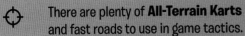

There are plenty of **All-Terrain Karts** and fast roads to use in game tactics.

Mats can be tricky to find in this large location.

The **Paradise Palms** desert is on the edge of the map, so if you land here make sure you're not caught out when the storm moves.

The **central shops** are tricky to loot because lots of players are around you and competing for weapons too.

The modern blocks of houses in Paradise Palms can be **confusing to navigate** from the inside. You'll need to master their layout and **work out the best loot paths** to collect chests and weapons.

The hotel is the tallest spot in the Paradise Palms desert. **Drop here to pick up lots of gear and goodies**, and possibly an easy kill from players lurking on the road below.

Dropping into the desert could force you to do lots of running to stay inside the **storm circle**. Keep watch for **sniper attacks** and, if you have time, harvest mats on the way to help you in the final phase.

The desert is full of red-hot fighting and chaos, but using one of the zone's many rifts will blast you into the sky and let you dive or glide somewhere else. **Rifts act like portals** that place you high above the spot they spawn.

Heading into the desert **junkyard** can be a risky strategy. You could harvest plenty of metal mats and reveal a chest, but if there are no karts or rifts around, you may face a race against the storm.

FOREST

Sunny Steps and Lonely Lodge are the two most popular forested locations. Other small wooded areas are dotted around.

- Head to the east of the island and practise in **Playground** mode to perfect your game in thick, forested areas.

- When the bush disguise item is in play, it blends in perfectly with wooded areas in the forest. Make sure you're not caught out when the storm moves.

- Mushrooms can be found in shady wooded areas and give **five shield** in just one second.

The mind-boggling **hedge maze** hides a chest.

Need guns and items right away? The shipping containers in Sunny Steps are the best source of weapons and goodies, but obviously the enemy will think that too - **firefights** in this clearing are very common!

Don't miss the **wooden watch tower** in Lonely Lodge - not that you will, because it's the tallest structure around! It can spawn multiple chests and set you up nicely for a shoot-out in the forest if you have a rifle and an accurate shot.

Remember that you can hide, heal and attack gamers from positions high up in the **tree canopy**. It can often be an unexpected move and it's hard for your target to shoot back as you're protected by the branches.

Scope out the forest floor for loot and opponents, but don't forget to go underground, too! The **bunker** in Wailing Woods is full of good stuff but be prepared to build your way out of it or use a **rift** to instantly escape.

Many Fortnite fans avoid spots like Wailing Woods and Lonely Lodge in Squads and Duos because they don't have enough chests to support a successful team. These zones are better suited to **Solo gameplay**.

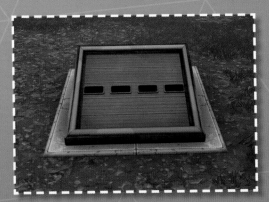

SNOW AND ICE

In season seven, snow and ice covered the south west of the map and created the Polar Peak, Frosty Flights and Happy Hamlet locations.

- Super slippery ice in Frosted Flights - keep your balance as you close in on the enemy!

- Choose Epic **zip lines** to cross the frozen surface (see page 141).

- Find **X-4 Stormwing planes** in Frosted Flights zone.

- Plane hangars and control centres stash plenty of loot.

From the Battle Bus, land at the **highest castle tower** that juts out from the snow (when the snow is freshly fallen) in Polar Peak. You'll have the high ground in any quick-fire combats, plus you can raid the tower for chests and cool weapons.

Don't worry if you're beaten to the top spot after landing on Polar Peak. The second-highest point has two towers to **launch attacks** from. In Duos or Squads, these two buildings could give you the edge over opponents camped at the top.

Just to the north of Frosted Flights is a small house with a thick forest around it. Raid the building for a chest, then start farming outside among the dense trees to boost your wood mats. You'll be ready for a **frozen fighting frenzy** after this!

Epic introduced the incredible **driftboard** to the icy landscape in a season seven update. This neat bit of kit allowed you to glide down glaciers and snow-covered hills in no time. Hit the **boost** button to power yourself into combat or away from danger!

The conditions are always changing in the **snow** and **ice biome**. The snow caps and icebergs can melt from day to day, meaning that previously hidden buildings suddenly come into play and you'll need to adjust your tactics. Pick **landing spots** carefully.

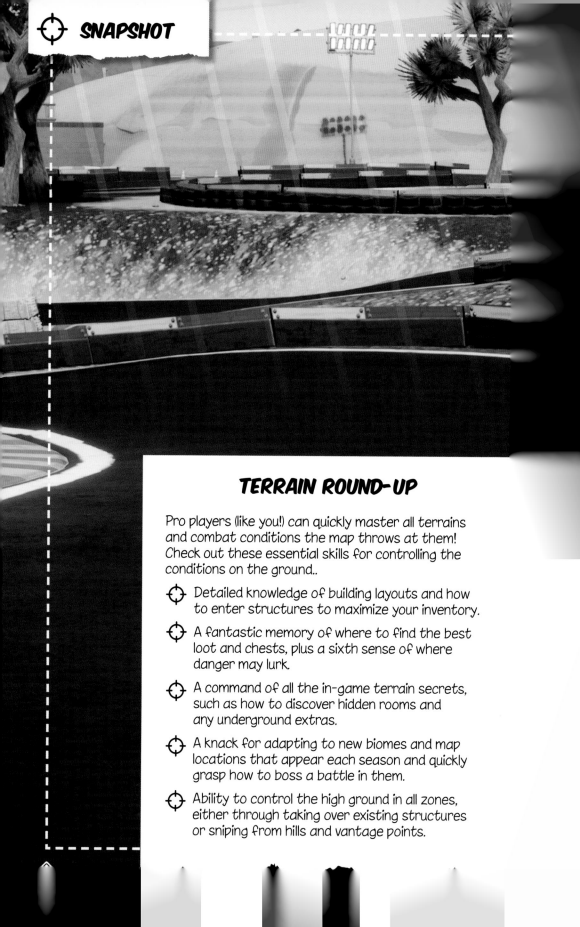

TERRAIN ROUND-UP

Pro players (like you!) can quickly master all terrains and combat conditions the map throws at them! Check out these essential skills for controlling the conditions on the ground..

- Detailed knowledge of building layouts and how to enter structures to maximize your inventory.

- A fantastic memory of where to find the best loot and chests, plus a sixth sense of where danger may lurk.

- A command of all the in-game terrain secrets, such as how to discover hidden rooms and any underground extras.

- A knack for adapting to new biomes and map locations that appear each season and quickly grasp how to boss a battle in them.

- Ability to control the high ground in all zones, either through taking over existing structures or sniping from hills and vantage points.

A ROYALE RIDE

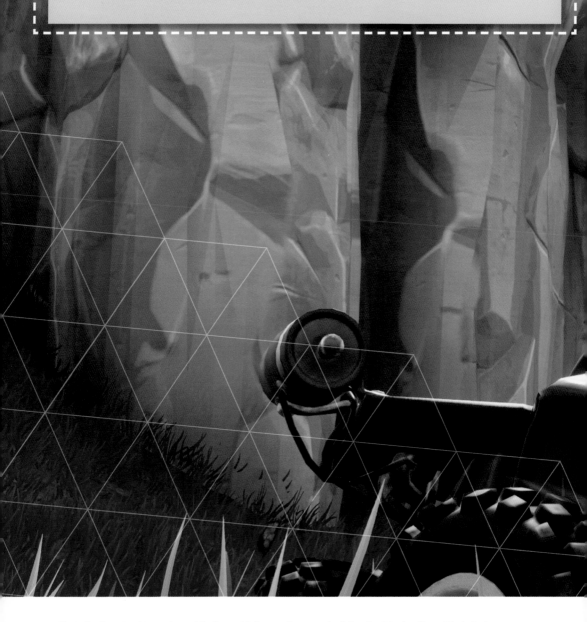

Fortnite fans had to wait a while for vehicles to drop on the island, with the first ride being the shopping cart back in season four! There are now several sick vehicles to cruise and crash around the zones - turn over for all the epic info.

X-4 STORMWING

One of the most adventurous Fortnite vehicles ever is actually found up in the skies, and not razzing around on the roads below. Say hello to the excellent X-4 Stormwing!

Experienced Battle Royale players know that the game's first proper flying vehicle (sadly you can't control the Battle Bus yourself!) was the **X-4.** It appeared in the snow and ice scenes of season seven and gamers scrambled to get behind the wheel of the crazy contraption!

The **X-4 Stormwing** could be found in **Frosty Flights,** around the hangar and control centre buildings, but it also spawned in other random spots on the map. This vehicle could zoom you into and away from combat, or fly through structures using **boost** without taking damage.

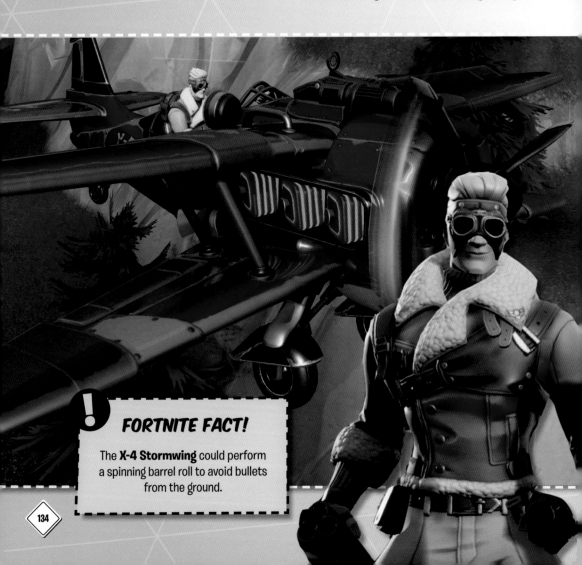

! FORTNITE FACT!

The **X-4 Stormwing** could perform a spinning barrel roll to avoid bullets from the ground.

Awesome Foursome

If you're in Squads, four other dudes could ride with you on the wings of the plane and shoot their weapons. Flying solo meant that you could **switch seats and fire** while the **X-4** carried on in its direction by itself. Nice.

Flying High

X-4 packed a high health of 800, meaning that it could take about **30 AR bullets** before it could even be shot down. If it was knocked out of the sky, anyone on board suffered 25 damage from the explosion.

Hot Stuff

The pilot needed to be very careful with the plane's weaponry because it **overheated if it was used for five or more seconds** at a time. Short and accurate burst fire was definitely the way to treat it.

All-TERRAIN KART

You've seen the All-Terrain Kart in action on page 119, but here you can really get to grips with this mega four-wheeled machine!

Bursting onto the map in the summer season five update, the **ATK** was a huge improvement from the shopping cart, which was the only other vehicle at that time. It became the perfect way to chase the enemy and escape the storm!

As well as being a fully-functional kart for combat moves, the **ATK** lets you pull off amazing drifts, slides and stunts over **roads**, **tracks**, **hills** and **grassland**. It even has a horn to press as you boss this cool kart.

FORTNITE FACT!

The roof of the **All-Terrain Kart** is also a bounce pad. Pretty neat!

Boost Power

Depending on the degree of slide you can achieve, you'll earn a **speed boost**. A small power drift with blue sparks underneath the **ATK** gives a low boost. A beefier blue spark slide makes you go faster, whereas the ultimate **yellow sparks really get you moving!**

Sound Stuff

Don't use the **ATK** if you're planning on a silent or sneaky attack on another squad. It's a super **noisy machine** that's designed to get you from place to place quickly, and to help you reach the final phase.

Rear Rockers

Not only can the rear passengers **help the ATK jump objects**, but the guys on the back can also **perform dances** (emotes) while the kart speeds along!

QUADCRASHER

The clue is in the name - the Quadcrasher smashes through structures and people and causes car-nage on the battlefield!

Revving into action during season six, the **Quadcrasher** delivered a new elimination tactic of driving into enemies and knocking them flying. In Solo mode or teaming up with your Duos buddy, the **Quad** can drive you into the endgame!

Like the **X-4** and **ATK,** the driver needs to build up boost to max out the **Quadcrasher's** speed. It storms through brick walls and if you're out of ammo, the bike can either become a weapon or your escape route to safety.

Awesome Air

The **Quadcrasher** can pretty much drive anywhere and with enough boost it'll climb hills and ramps. Launch it from the cliff edge and collect some sick air time with your **sky-high stunts**.

Divide and Conquer

A good tactic in Duos is to use the **Quadcrasher** to break through the base of ramps and forts on their own, while the other player **snipes and shoots** the enemy from mid range.

Water Surprise

With your Duo player on the back, the **Quadcrasher** can speed across water. The rear passenger just needs to build a wooden path as you journey along. It's a **top tactic** and looks mega cool!

MAKING A MOVE

Not all of these are strictly vehicles, but they are essential ways to cover ground and get the drop on your Fortnite foes.

Shopping Cart

Jump on a **cart** and make up ground on the storm, closing in on enemy targets... or just have a laugh cruising the map! **One player** can push the **cart** in Solos and a second can jump inside, but with 400 health it doesn't protect you from weapons much.

Smart Duos let the passenger shoot at other players while the driver steers a safe path over ground. **Carts** can usually handle going downhill on cliff edges and have some collision protection when smashed into structures.

Double Trouble

Even **noobs** know that gliders are deployed when you skydive from the Bus! But they have become an important **in-game item** too, thanks to re-deploy and launchpads.

If a launchpad is used to **propel** you up into the air, your glider can steer you to where you want to land. In season six, **glider re-deploy** allowed it to open if a player jumps from a height of three storeys or more. Gliders help you to travel the map much quicker than by foot.

Zip Line

When the snow swept into the south in season seven, **zip lines** also appeared around the map as a fun way to travel to and from high ground. All you had to do was jump underneath the **zip line** post and a **magnet** attached you to the line and **set you moving**.

Players could perform multi functions while travelling the **zip line** - weapons and inventory items were at your disposal. It became a top tactic for **sniping the oppo**, but it also made you a target as you swung freely in the air.

Balloons

Gamers can hold as many as **six Epic rarity balloons**, so they are able to rise up and drop into battles and buildings with ease. Make a silent move on the enemy by ballooning and appearing right behind them!

If you spot the balloon item in floor loots, Supply Llamas, Vending Machines and chests. Have a go at inflating with the **primary fire** button and check out the distance they can carry you. Don't float too high or too long though, as they become ineffective at the maximum build height.

VEHICLE ROUND-UP

Sliding over the ground, rocketing down roads and soaring into the sky are all possible with Fortnite's fantastic vehicles. Expert battlers must master these skills behind the wheel...

- Control a range of machines and the hotkeys that get the most from them.

- Use the right vehicle at the right time for attacking and defensive situations.

- Let your duo or squad do deadly damage with weapons while you steer or drive.

- Know where to locate the vehicles on the map and keep them operating.

- Know the damage that driving and flying machines can inflict on the opposition and the best way to maximize that.

BE CREATIVE!

The launch of Fortnite Creative was one of the **biggest updates of all time**. It gives players the chance to build their own islands, create cool landscapes, have fun games and unique Battle Royales. It doesn't matter if you're a pro or a beginner - jump in and get creative!

7 THINGS TO KNOW ABOUT
FORTNITE CREATIVE

Creative hit the scene in season seven, so check out our
seven super tips and stats all about this fascinating Fortnite mode.

Use 'My Island' in
the Main Menu to share
and change settings.

1 The **phone** is your **most important tool** in Creative. It has the power to **rotate, build, push, pull, drop, manipulate** and **edit** whatever you decide to make appear on your island.

2 Three **other gamers** can join you in your **pre-Creative mode lobby**. At launch in season seven, 12 more friends could come to your island, meaning 16 friends can go crazy and have fun together.

3 You can support you **favourite creators** by entering the code they share on one of the four **featured maps** in the hub. This will take you to a cool custom world and game.

4 You have the power to **fly** in Fortnite Creative! No, not like Superman, but the fly mode carries you to **any spot** so that you can build and edit what you want and where you want it from.

5 Watch the **memory bar** at the bottom of the screen. This shows the game storage you have. There's also a **countdown clock** for your session... but when it runs out, you can just jump right back in and carry on.

6 Fortnite Creative was developed by Epic with the help of loads of YouTubers, creators and community leaders. The likes of **Lachlan, Bajan** and **Rifty** had an early test and helped Epic to make it even more special!

7 From the Creative hub you can join one of **four featured islands**, your own islands, or those from the other 15. Your rift glows orange and can take you to any of your four **saved zones**.

COOLEST CREATIVE STUFF

We've done your Fortnite homework and picked out the most mega things from the cool Creative mode. Check out this bunch of sick stuff!

ZONE CLONE

The prefabs tab has stacks of buildings and structures. Many of these have been taken from the regular Battle Royale map, so you can place **scary buildings** from Haunted Hills right next to a shop or house from another location. Top idea!

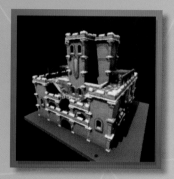

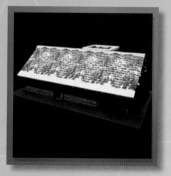

BOSS THE OBS

The moment Creative mode dropped in Fortnite, its obstacle courses and events became ultra popular. Structures can be plucked from the **prefabs tab** and stuck on your island to be raced and climbed against friends in manic mini games.

CREATE COMBAT

Creative lets you have a laugh with your friends, but there's also a semi-serious side to combat mini games. Choose how many teams will take to the battlefield, loot your weapons and **get the game on** as you hunt the oppo in **quick-fire** action.

FAME GAME

One of Epic's first special features that **encouraged creative builds** was The Block. The Block was a special area on the Battle Royale map where a handful of the coolest Creative structures were displayed. Epic also gave these gamers a big in-game and social media shout-out!

AMAZING AMMO

Creative really lets you try stuff that's not possible in a usual Fortnite game. Some players love having the **infinite ammo option** selected and others hate it, but it deffo makes for spectacular private island games!

WHAT A SHOCK

There's a bunch of blingin' new items in Creative that aren't in the normal game. Vehicle spawn pads, speed pads and ice block traps are neat, but the **electric shock rails** spice your obstacle and race games right up. They cause five damage each time you buzz into them.

GUN FUN

Every weapon that's currently playable in Battle Royale can be selected for action in Creative mode. So, if you reckon the burst AR, the tactical shotgun or the quad launcher will do the deadly business, **select them and get 'em on your island!**

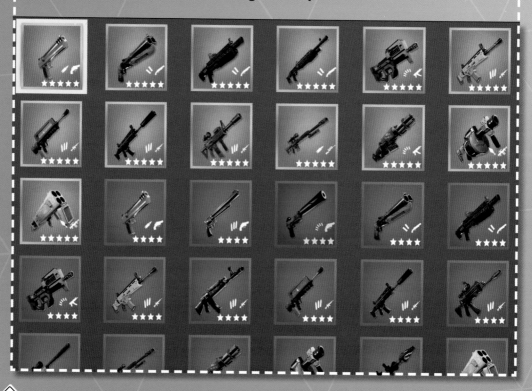

GET CHANGED

In the '**My Island**' tab, the tools setting can be selected so that either only the island creator, or the other players who can appear there, can edit what's on the island. It's a way to protect your creations and make sure that no one breaks and spoils your slick structures!

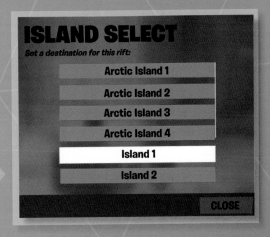

ISLAND SELECT

Set a destination for this rift:

Arctic Island 1

Arctic Island 2

Arctic Island 3

Arctic Island 4

Island 1

Island 2

CLOSE

SPAM THE PLAN

You'll find that many gamers in Creative will hit the **spam** button and repeat place something they really like. You can stick ten Quadcrashers in a row, 18 buses upside down or a huge line of, er, bushes!

BEST CHESTS

Have you always wanted to pack your own chests and decide which loot and weapons can be hidden inside? You can do exactly that in Creative! You can stuff an Epic **SCAR** and **chug jug** inside each one if you wish. Loot Llamas can also be packed with crazy gear.

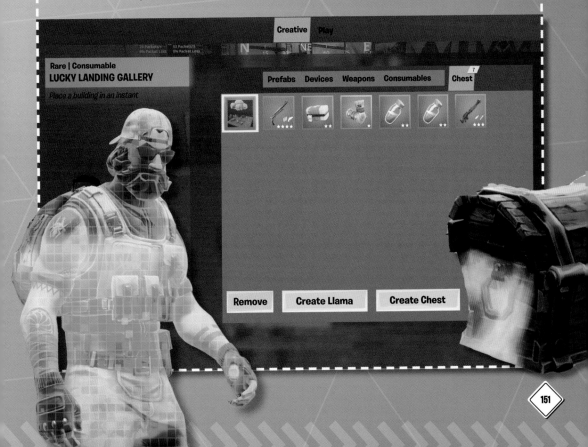

CREATIVE ROUND-UP

Creative isn't essential in helping you to become a top star on the battlefield, but it'll fine-tune your gameplay and tactics. Take a peek at what mastering this mode will mean for you...

⊕ Boost your imagination and develop building powers beyond the limits of normal play.

⊕ Help you to think in different ways and react instantly to strange situations, abilities and moves.

⊕ Improve your team play and group tactics around the tight field of the smaller island.

⊕ Sharpen up shooting skills because of close combat in quick mini games.

⊕ Tackle environments and obstacles built by the game's best creators when you enter a code and join the rift of featured islands.

EXPERT ESSENTIALS

In this section you'll meet the most amazing Fortnite pros of all time! These players are brilliant Battle Royale heroes on YouTube and Twitch. Discover why millions of fans follow them and watch their videos for expert tips and tactics.

BATTLE STARS

Ninja

Real name: Tyler Blevins
Born: 5 June, 1991
Lives: US
YouTube subscribers: 22 million +
Twitch followers: 14 million +

FORTNITE FACT!

Ninja is thought to earn around $500,000 each month through Fortnite streams and adverts watched on his YouTube channel.

The sickest Fortnite pro player of all time is **Ninja**. He's a **YouTube phenomenon** with millions of fans watching his Twitch streams and YouTube videos each week. Ninja has been a streamer since 2009 with games like Halo and PUBG, but switched to Fortnite in 2017. He's been part of Luminosity, Team Liquid, Renegades, and Cloud9 gaming teams.

Ninja says he plays Fortnite for **10 to 12 hours** a day. He usually has a six-hour session which begins in the morning, and he then takes a long break before streaming again in the evening.

Ninja always stresses that Fortnite should be a **fun hobby for young fans** - not many people can afford to play for as long as he does! He wants his followers to work hard at school first, then maybe play for an hour or two if their parents allow it.

His top tip is to keep practising and to keep landing in busy locations to test your skills against opponents.

Nick EH 30

- -

Real name: Nicholas Amyoony
Born: 14 March, 1995
Lives: US
YouTube subscribers: 4.5 million +
Twitch followers: 97,000 +

This Canadian gamer is big mates with Ninja and their deadly Duo match-ups get millions of views! **Nick EH 30** is an expert eliminator and an epic team player, plus this dude is awesome in Solos. He's famed for his **building skills**, so if you want legendary creating and editing tips, try his videos.

DanTDM

- -

Real name: Daniel Middleton
Born: 8 November, 1991
Lives: UK
YouTube subscribers: 21 million +
Twitch followers: 210,000 +

UK gamers will know all about **DanTDM** - he's the most epic British gamer ever! He's a fan of several video games, such as Minecraft, Skylanders and Rocket League, and he regularly uploads Fortnite YouTube content. He'll admit that he's not the best Battle Royale fighter in the world, but he's still a sweet player with **hundreds of Victory Royales**. DanTDM's a funny vlogger and gamer, so be sure to catch his cool vids now!

Ali-A

- - - - - - - - - - - - - - - - -

Real name: Alistair Aiken
Born: 6 November, 1993
Lives: UK
YouTube subscribers: 16 million +
Twitch followers: 230,000 +

Ali-A is a YouTube hero and a legend to Fortnite fans! His followers love how he explains new updates and features (such as the Cube in season six) and he provides expert tips and strategies. If you reach the top ten, Ali-A's advice is to count the others left and to know where they are. Try counting the forts built, and then work through eliminating each one.

iBallisticSquid

- - - - - - - - - - - - - - - - - - - -

Real name: David Spencer
Born: 29 January, 1992
Lives: UK
YouTube subscribers: 4.2 million +
Twitch followers: 55,000 +

Tutorials, builds, tactics and laughs – **iBallisticSquid** offers all of this to his huge army of Fortnite followers. The Yorkshireman, who has an unmistakable high-pitched voice, vlogs about Minecraft, but he's become a big hit on the Battle Royale scene too. iBallisticSquid is an original Fortnite player from 2017, so give this guy total respect!

Typical Gamer

- - - - - - - - - - - - - - - - - - - -

Real name: Andre Rebelo
Born: 23 March, 1992
Lives: UK
YouTube subscribers: 8.3 million +
Twitch followers: 125,000 +

Search for **Typical Gamer**'s Fortnite videos and you could spend hours admiring his awesome online skills! The Canadian is deffo one of the best in the business and he is a weapons expert and brilliant builder. Typical Gamer also posts clips playing driving videogames – he loves showing off his sick Lamborghini, which is way faster than an ATK!

SypherPK

- - - - - - - - - - - - - - - - - - - -

Real name: Ali Hassan
Born: 10 May, 1996
Lives: US
YouTube subscribers: 1.7 million +
Twitch followers: 2.4 million +

If you're a good Fortnite gamer but you want to become great, then check out **SypherPK** on YouTube and Twitch. He's got the skills to join the top Duos and Squads in the world, but the best thing about SypherPK are his educational vids. He's fantastic at explaining the moves that he makes and how he clinches Victory Royales, plus how to get the most from updates. Watch and learn!

KingRichard

Real name: Richard Nelson
Born: 11 January, 1989
Lives: US
YouTube subscribers: 240,000 +
Twitch followers: 1.4 million +

KingRichard reigns on the island. This pro player clocked up a staggering 32 kills in Solos versus Squads in 2018! That year he was also named captain of the NRG eSports team and he's a powerhouse online gamer. KingRichard has a huge army of Twitch followers who show up daily to see his combat and sniping skills. Take a look at this ruthless operator.

Mongraal

Real name: Kyle Jackson
Born: 12 August, 2004
Lives: UK
YouTube subscribers: 1.8 million +
Twitch followers: 1.4 million +

Be sure to you check out **Mongraal's** channels, as this teen is probably the best young Fortnite player on Earth! In Duos or Solos he can wipe out guys twice his age, and he practises all day in the school holidays. Mongraal joined Team Secret's Fortnite Squad in 2018 and no doubt he'll be one of the hottest full-time pros when he's an adult.

dakotaz

Real name: Brett Hoffman
Born: 12 July, 1986
Lives: France
YouTube subscribers: 3 million +
Twitch followers: 3.9 million +

There's one reason why Fornite fans watch **dakotaz** and that's sniping! He streams daily on Twitch and displays the most awesome long-range shooting ability. Dakotaz is unbelievable with assault rifles and will lock onto a headshot from distances that other gamers can only dream of. View his vids for super helpful sniping tips.

9 THINGS TO KNOW!

FORTNITE ESPORTS

Fortnite's Battle Royale mode is a top title in the world of professional gaming. Check out these eSports facts!

1   **eSports** means competitive gaming tournaments - basically, a bunch of awesome Fortnite players battle against each other for **prizes**, **trophies** and **gaming glory**! For the first Fortnite eSports season, Epic handed out **$100 million** in prize money.

2 Anyone can get involved and you don't have to be an elite player or have zillions of **YouTube** subs! Some events are online where players qualify and compete from home, while others are held in arenas so that fans can come to watch or follow on streams.

3 The Fortnite **2018 Summer Skirmish Series** was the debut official Battle Royale **eSports** competition. It's for Duos and involves the winners needing to notch up two Victory Royales. US stars '**Kevie1**' and '**NotVivid**' were victorious!

4

In season six, Fortnite revealed the new **In-Game Tournaments**, accessed through the events section in Battle Royale. Players are matched with others of similar ability and earn points by high placements or eliminations collected.

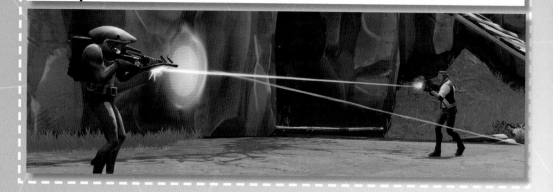

5

The 2018 **Fall Skirmish** followed the **Summer Skirmish** series. Around 500 gamers were divided into five teams called **Fort Knights, Lucky Llamas, Dusty Dogs, Rift Raiders** and **Bush Bandits**.

| FORT KNIGHTS | LUCKY LLAMAS | DUSTY DOGS | RIFT RAIDERS | BUSH BANDITS |

6

Netherlands-based eSports outfit Team Liquid has quickly become a major Fortnite force. Squad members '**Poach**', '**72hrs**' and '**Chap**' all tasted Battle Royale success in the Skirmish tournaments. These boys mean business on the island!

7 During the first **Summer Skirmish** games in 2018, nearly **500** Fortnite community members picked up cash prizes. GG, guys!

8 It took until 2019 for the first Fortnite **World Cup competition** to take place at the end of 2019, after qualifiers around the world.

9 **In-Game Tournaments** are designed for Solos, Duos and Squads. When the competition kicked off there were three trophies up for grabs: **Salty Spring Cup** (Solo), **Tomato Temple Cup** (Duos) and **Friday Night Fortnite** (Squads).

SALTY SPRING CUP

TOMATO TEMPLE CUP

FRIDAY NIGHT FORTNITE

! FORTNITE FACT!

The 8-series **Summer Skirmish** saw **$8 million** in prize money awarded to gamers.

EXPERT ROUND-UP

Even if you have a hundred Victory Royales, you can always learn from the guys and girls who play the game professionally. Studying and watching YouTube and eSports stars can teach you stacks of stuff...

- When new seasons and updates drop, discover how the elite use new weapons and items.

- Pick up tactics from the best and use them when you lead your Squad teams on the island.

- Building is essential for reaching the top ten and the world's best crafters reveal their secrets on YouTube and Twitch.

- You'll never miss a piece of news, such as new skins and emotes, because the pros always discuss these on their channels.

- Get step-by-step guides on Battle Passes and how to progress and earn rewards.

LETHAL LOLS!

Millions of fans take their battles super seriously, but you can still share a laugh and a joke about Fortnite as well. Get ready for gaming giggles, including dances, memes and gags!

EPIC EMOTES

Get down with the grooviest guide to the deadliest dances in Fortnite!

FLOSS

From grannies to babies, it feels like **every person on the planet** knows about the Floss! It's the most famous Fortnite routine of all time.

Dance directions: Arms by your side with fists clenched. Swing them from side to side around your body in the opposite direction to your hips, with one in front and one behind you. Now repeat this in the other direction, but swing your arms in front of you. Easy, eh?!

FORTNITE FACT!

The Floss was part of the Battle Pass back in season two.

FREESTYLIN'

This flashy sequence was created to get gamers ripping up the dance floor! It has Epic rarity and it was first released to Twitch Prime subscribers.

Dance directions: Begin by dropping and bending both knees, then raising your right knee and swinging both arms low. Ripple your body to the left, then the right. Slam your right fist down, followed by your left and beat a pretend drum that's low down in front of you!

ZANY

It's a little weird, it's a little fresh and it's totally... zany! This move is short, bouncy and all about the jazz hands.

Dance directions: Stamp each foot in turn, keeping your arms tucked by your side with a bouncy beat through your body. Stamp your feet together, clench your fists into a ball and then flick out your fingers while raising your right foot and looking to your right.

SWIPE IT

This Rare emote was in high demand during the season five Battle Pass in 2018. 'Swipe it over and over again' was the official tag from Epic!

Dance directions: Get your knees swaying side to side. Place your right arm out low to the side, palm facing forward, then pull it back towards your left shoulder and spin your hands around each other. Swipe each hand forward separately as if you're waving a pesky wasp away!

DISCO FEVER

Described by Epic as a move that heats up the dance floor, Disco Fever gets your arms, legs, hips and fingers in full swing. It's funky and fresh, y'all!

Dance directions: Bounce and wag your fingers to your right, then to the left. Point your arm straight and to your right, then pull it back across yourself while bopping. Raise your right arm up above your head, then pop it on your left hip and back up again.

YOU'RE AWESOME

Don't try this unless you're a brilliant gymnast and very flexible! You'll need to do the splits and pop back up on your feet in a split second.

Dance directions: Begin by being side-on to your audience. Raise your right knee up, then swing it back behind you and do the splits. Pull your legs back together to stand up, spin round twice and finally, point to the crowd. Awesome!

WORK IT OUT

This is one for aerobic fans and it was a red-hot smash when it hit the item shop in the summer of 2018. It may be simple, but it can work up a sweat.

Dance directions: Run on the spot and clap, then bounce to your left and right with elbows pointed out. Spin round and keep your arms in a 'T' pose. Finish off with a simple high, overarm reach with each arm and raise your right knee while punching the air.

ROCK, PAPER, SCISSORS

This old-school hand game has become a classic dance move on the island. It's also one of the easiest - get this wrong and you don't deserve to be playing Fortnite!

Dance directions: Best performed with your Duos' teammate after a Victory Royale, just tap your fist against your other hand three times while crouched forward. Then, unleash the rock, paper or scissors sign with your hand. Game on, dudes!

FRESH

Named after a famous US TV show called *The Fresh Prince of Bel-Air*, this is a royal Royale move of the highest order...

Dance directions: Keep your body facing forward and swing both arms high to your left, then to your right, twice. Take a step to the right and snap your arms together at the same time. Repeat that going the other way and you're a 'fresh' dancer!

TRUE HEART

If you're truly in love with Battle Royale, you'll want to learn this funky Fortnite routine. It's a tough one that needs plenty of pro practice.

Dance directions: Search for the full routine online. To finish, have both arms raised straight up and begin to lower them while swaying your hips and rocking your arms from side to side. Then jump and tap your right arm to your right heel. Finally, draw a big heart with both hands.

BREAKIN'

Take a break from it all and kick back with these classic moves. You'll have to embrace your inner gymnast to really pull them off though.

Dance directions: To ace these moves IRL will take time. Check out breakdancing videos online and start with the easier downrock moves. When you've found your rhythm, step it up a gear with power moves and a fearsome freeze to finish on!

BOOGIE DOWN

Get some tunes blasting out and limber up for this fun, fast Emote that's part-skipping and part-funk!

Dance directions: The key to this dance is keep your feet moving. Alternate between pretending to skip with an imaginary rope and kicking out to the left and the right.

SHIMMER

Tap your toes and flex those wrists for your Shimmer to really shine. Pick a song with a good beat and step up to the moves...

Dance directions: Move your left leg forward and back in time to the music while waving your arms in the air. Rotate your hands at the wrist for added flair. Now swap legs - forward and back with the right leg, but don't forget those hand and arm moves, too!

SALUTE

DAB

RIDE THE PONY

BRUSH YOUR SHOULDERS

FORTNITE FUNNIES!

The world is full of Fortnite LOLs and jokes. Check out the best gaming gags and giggles...

You're a Joke, Dude!

Which music star do Fortnite fans hate?
Storm-zy!

Why were 100 cows flying in the air?
They jumped from the Cattle Bus!

Why did tadpoles suddenly appear on the map?
Because of frogs-spawning!

Why did the Fortnite players land in just their underwear?
They were playing out of their skin!

Why did the emergency services drop into the island?
Because someone set off the fire llama!

Essential Emojis

I WAS THE FIRST ELIMINATED AND HAVE TO WAIT FOR MY SQUAD.

STAY LOW, MOVE SLOW... UNLEASH A SURPRISE AMBUSH SHOW!

I GOT THE ROCKET LAUNCHER!

WHEN FORTNITE LAGS... AT 2ND PLACE!

SAY WHAT?!

When Fortnite was first launched and gamers (and parents!) began talking about the game, many of them thought it was called **Fork Knife**. LOL! Epic found this so funny that they soon displayed it on the side of a red food truck!

SMG LOCKED AND LOADED. LEAVE THIS TO ME, TEAM.

FORTNITE SERVER DOWN ALL WEEKEND? SERIOUSLY UNFUNNY.

I GOT V-BUCKS FOR MY BIRTHDAY, DUDES!!!

NOT. FEELING. GOOD. NEED. MEDS. NOW!

BATTLE ROYALE:
BEST BITS EVER!

Gameplay is constantly updated and changing in Fortnite, so check out some of the best bits you may have missed!

Perfect Pets

Like skins, **pets** are only a cosmetic item and don't improve your kill count in any way... but they look awesome! Similar to **back bling**, they react to what's going on in the game and become your loyal companion. **Bonesy**, **Camo** and **Scales** are sick creatures!

Golden Glory

Imagine how cool it would be if all weapons on the map were Legendary. The landscape would be full of golden assault rifles, miniguns, heavy shotguns and bolt-action snipers. Well, that's exactly what happens when Epic unleashes the **Solid Gold Limited Time Mode** (LTM). It's absolutely awesome and a total firearm fest!

High-powered

Don't forget this sick move, which was first released in season six. In Solo, Duo and Squad mode, players can **re-deploy their glider** if they are at least **three storeys high**. It makes for a quick escape from the enemy and covering ground in a matter of seconds.

Boogie Time

You gotta get on down when the **Boogie Bomb** strikes! Use this Rare item to throw at your opponent, and anyone caught in the blast is **forced to dance** for five seconds. It's mega funny, but it also gives the thrower time to plan their next move and inflict some damage. Time to dance, dudes!

Football Fashion

Love Fortnite? Love NFL? Epic created these sick NFL skins in November 2018 featuring **all 32 American football teams**. Players rushed the item shop like a pro running back as soon as they came out!

Shadow Stones

Appearing in spooky season six (just in time for Halloween) **shadow stones** were an Epic item. They allowed the user to change into shadow form and become invisible when standing still. It lasted for 45 seconds, but weapons couldn't be used during this time.

Happy Halloween

Okay, so the **pumpkin launcher** was only a visual change to the rocket launcher and carried no extra power. But when it's Halloween and you're bossing a battle by blasting pumpkins in Fortnitemares, you're gonna be a legend!

Quality Quad

An explosive item that can help you take that vital Victory Royale, the **quad launcher** is a fearsome foursome firearm! Blast up to four rockets quickly, with a reload time of 4.5 seconds. They'll deliver 80 or 84 damage and over 300 structure damage. Epic, hey?

DESIGN TIME:

DREAM UP YOUR OWN STUFF!

Imagine how incredible it would be to have your own skins, weapons and vehicles in Fortnite! These pages will help you to think of sick stuff you'd like to see appear...

Grab a separate piece of paper and some pencils, pens and a ruler, and begin to sketch out your Fortnite ideas. As well as machines and outfits, what items and extras could be in the game? You could even **draw your ultimate fort** or map out a new island!

Share your sketches with your friends and see what they think of your designs. Maybe one day you'll end up being a designer for Epic Games and having the **coolest job** on the planet!

Super Skin

You will have seen hundreds of player skins in Battle Royale, but which ones did you think were **extra awesome**? You can borrow ideas from those and try adding personal touches of your own. Maybe include your school uniform, fave footy team or a superhero outfit.

Wonder Weapon

What are the **best bits about your no.1 weapon**? Maybe you love scoped sights or love firing from the hip at speed? Will it be a shotgun, an RPG or an explosive item? On your paper, draw the deadliest weapon that you think will wipe out the enemy!

Rockin' Ride

Quadcrashers, Stormwings, Karts, trolleys... You've ridden them all, so how can you dream up an even more **lethal vehicle**? Perhaps a ride that can handle the road, water *and* take to the skies is what Fortnite really needs? Sketch a wicked vehicle that will totally boss the whole map.

FORTNITE QUIZ
TEST YOUR
BATTLE ROYALE BRAIN
The answers are on page 192!

1 In a fight with the enemy, what does CQC mean?

A. Close quarters combat
B. Clear quarters combat
C. Clever quest chase

2 Which colours represent each of the weapon rarities?

Common
Uncommon
Rare
Epic
Legendary

3 What was Tomato Temple previously called?

A. Tomato City
B. Tomato Town
C. Town Tomato

4 Which of these has the biggest magazine size?

A. Compact SMG
B. Hand cannon
C. Bolt-action sniper rifle

5 What's the maximum time a Cosy Campfire will last?

A. 30 minutes
B. 40 seconds
C. 25 seconds

6 With weaponry, what does DPS mean?

A. Damage per second
B. Double pump shotgun
C. Damage per shotgun

7 Which of these is best for close-range battles?

A. Assault rifle
B. Pistol
C. Shotgun

8 In which year was Fortnite Battle Royale first released?

A. 2006
B. 2015
C. 2017

MY FORTNITE FACT FILE

>>>>> <<<<<

Keep a record of your kills, Victory Royales, faves, facts and stats from the battlefield!

My age:

My name:

Year I started playing Fortnite:

Fave weapon:

....

Fave explosive:

....

I play Duos with:

....

Fave location to land:

....

My skills (rated out of 10):

Shooting ..../10

Sniping ..../10

Looting ..../10

Building ..../10

Teamwork.............../10

Most kills in a game:

....

I have .... Victory Royales

I play Squads with:

....

Fave skin:

....

....

....

ANSWERS

1   In a fight with the enemy, what does CQC mean?

A. Close quarters combat

2   Which colours represent each of the weapon rarities?

Common = **grey**
Uncommon = **green**
Rare = **blue**
Epic = **purple**
Legendary = **orange/gold**

3   What was Tomato Temple previously called?

B. Tomato Town

4   Which of these has the biggest magazine size?

A. Compact SMG

5   What's the maximum time a Cosy Campfire will last?

C. 25 seconds

6   With weaponry, what does DPS mean?

A. Damage per second

7   Which of these is best for close-range battles?

C. Shotgun

8   In which year was Fortnite Battle Royale first released?

C. 2017